# MILTON'S PASTORAL VISION

# MILTON'S PASTORAL VISION

## An Approach to *Paradise Lost*

John R. Knott, Jr. 

THE UNIVERSITY OF CHICAGO PRESS
Chicago and London

*International Standard Book Number: 0–226–44846–0*
*Library of Congress Catalog Card Number: 79–145576*

The University of Chicago Press, Chicago 60637
The University of Chicago Press, Ltd., London


*Published 1971*
*Printed in the United States of America*

*For Anne*

# CONTENTS

# ACKNOWLEDGMENTS

Douglas Bush and Herschel Baker started me thinking about Milton and gave generously of their kind and shrewd counsel and their considerable learning when this study was in its early stages. One chapter benefited from the suggestions of Arnold Stein, the whole manuscript from a careful and sympathetic reading by Joseph Summers. To my colleague, Frank Huntley, that sociable spirit, I owe special thanks for a painstaking reading of the manuscript and for continuing encouragement and friendship. Many of those who have written on Milton in recent years have shaped my thinking in important ways; they will recognize how substantial my debt to them is. I am grateful to the Canaday Fund for the Humanities of Harvard University and to the Horace H. Rackham School of Graduate Studies of the University of Michigan for summer grants that gave me valuable free time. My greatest debt is to my wife, who is a good critic and, more important, continues to make it all worthwhile.

Chapter 2 is reprinted from *Milton Studies*, vol. 2 (1970), edited by James M. Simmonds, by permission of the University of Pittsburgh Press. Chapter 3 is reprinted from *PMLA* 85 (1970), by permission of the Modern Language Association of America. Chapter 4 appeared in *Modern Language Quarterly* 29 (1968), and is reprinted by permission.

# PREFACE

IN HIS ELEGY COMMEMORATING THE DEATH OF HIS FRIEND Charles Diodati, Milton announced his plans to write an Arthurian epic and at the same time promised to hang his shepherd's pipe on a pine tree. Nothing could have been more natural than a gesture of this sort for a Renaissance poet of Milton's talent and ambition. Virgil had established the pattern, imitated by Spenser and others, of serving a literary apprenticeship in pastoral poetry before attempting the noblest and most demanding genre, the epic. When Milton finally came to write his epic, over twenty years later, he had left pastoral poetry far behind him.

His chosen subject demanded drastic modifications of the conventions of the classical epic and a reinterpretation of its purposes. Much of the criticism of *Paradise Lost* has been devoted to showing how Milton justified his argument by reorienting the epic toward the combat of God and man with Satan and the kind of heroism exemplified by Christ and the repentant Adam. But Milton's subject prompted another innovation no less remarkable from the standpoint of epic tradition: the elevation of scenes in a predominantly pastoral mode to a position of critical importance. When Milton made the earthly paradise rather than the battlefield the main stage for the action of his epic, he replaced heroic values with others that can be characterized as pastoral. I am not suggesting that Milton returned in spirit or in style to the pastoral exercises of his early career or that he is guilty of a confusion of genres. At least since Sidney voiced his contempt for "mongrel tragi-comedy" critics have intently guarded the purity of genres. But the very habit of thinking in terms of genres with fixed conventions may blind one to the fact that *Paradise Lost* is an epic with a pastoral center. Milton did not abandon the pastoral mode when he stopped writing elegies and masques.

We may think of Eden as Milton's rendering of the earthly paradise and not recognize it as a version of Arcadia. Yet his presentation of the life of Adam and Eve in paradise strongly recalls the idealized world that appears in a variety of forms in classical pastoral poetry and in Renaissance pastoral lyrics, eclogues, masques, dramas, and romances. Milton's Eden is much more Arcadian, in fact, than that of other works dealing with the fall of man, most of which have little to say about the manner of life in paradise. It combines conventional features of the earthly paradise with a host of familiar pastoral motifs accommodated to Milton's Christian vision. The harmony of Adam and Eve with their environment, the responsiveness of nature to their moods, the *otium* that they enjoy, the natural rhythm of their day, and the innocence of their love all owe a great deal to pastoral tradition. But for such obvious landmarks of the earthly paradise as golden fruit and thornless roses, the Garden itself—with hills and dales, arbors, bowers, and flocks—could be mistaken for Arcadia.

Milton's subject matter enabled him to simplify further an already simple ideal of pastoral life by avoiding such conventional preoccupations of the eclogue as singing matches and love complaints. By introducing God and the angels into Arcadia (the pagan gods linger only in the imagination, summoned by allusions), Milton was able to broaden the scope of pastoral and give it a new seriousness. We can regard the joy of the senses as holy and the repose of Adam and Eve as proof of their obedience because Eden is the Garden of God. In *Paradise Lost* the simple life, removed from the vices and confusions of society, becomes a means of knowing God and the unity of all creation and of realizing the fullest communion with the divine possible in this life. By grounding the Arcadian ideal in what he regarded as theological reality, Milton could present it as the model for human happiness established by God and not merely as a sophisticated literary fiction.

Within the framework of *Paradise Lost* the final authority for the ideal of pastoral simplicity is the life of the angels in their celestial paradise. Although Milton copied significant details from the New Jerusalem of the Book of Revelation, he boldly emphasized the pastoral aspect of heaven, so that the bliss of Adam and Eve truly seems a "shadow" of that of the angels. Because the angels sit in their "fellowships of joy" in a landscape of bowers and fountains, heavenly perfection conforms at least in part to an ideal that we can recognize. Even the angelic hymns of celebration can be regarded as a higher and more ecstatic version of the pastoral hymns of Adam and Eve.

Much of the power of *Paradise Lost* arises from the fact that the pastoral center of the poem will not hold; Milton's vision of an ideal pastoral life on earth dissolves in the face of Satan's assault and man's subsequent sin. Spenser had suggested the limitations of pastoral life by playing it off against demands for heroic action and the real dangers that threaten the stability of any form of human society. Brigands leave the Arcadian world of Pastorella in ruins (though Calidore is able to restore her to her noble parents and the society in which she belongs). In *Paradise Lost* the pastoral state is not a refuge but a mode of existence lost irrevocably by the act of disobeying God. Milton's pastoral vision involves a simplicity, a moral purity, and a degree of harmony with God and nature that would be inconceivable in the fallen world.

The movement of *Paradise Lost* depends upon a continuous interaction of pastoral and epic modes. In reading Book I, perhaps the book closest to the classical epic in spirit, we are reminded of the "peace" and "rest" that the fallen angels formerly enjoyed in the "happy Fields" of heaven. Milton undermined whatever heroism and splendor he granted Satan and his armies by implicitly comparing their militarism with the paradisal life of heaven. Heaven has its armies too, but they serve God and not personal ambition. The epic and pastoral modes can coexist in heaven because Milton uses the former to express God's power and the latter his peace.

Eden appears in the poem as an island in the sea of space highly vulnerable to assault by the forces of hell. Although Satan comes in disguise and accomplishes his victory through fraud, he comes as a conqueror bent on enlarging his empire to spite God. Once hellish power threatens the fragile bliss of paradise, there can be little doubt about the outcome. The very conflict of modes, epic against pastoral, seems to doom Eden in advance. With the arrival of Sin and Death paradise is finally engulfed by the power of hell, as if absorbed into the epic mode.

Even after the Fall, though, Eden serves as a moral center against which traditional assumptions about heroism and the proper end of human activities are tested. If the growth of great cities and civilizations is seen as a movement away from an ideal simplicity, as Milton represents it, then whatever glory nations and individuals achieve on earth is illusory. The violence and moral corruption that accompany the expansion of civil power can be judged by the peaceful, virtuous life of Adam and Eve.

By their sin Adam and Eve condemn themselves and their descendants to a prolonged combat with the world, the flesh, and the devil that constitutes a new kind of spiritual epic. The recovery of peace, the "paradise within" that Michael promises Adam, depends upon a radical simplification of one's inner life through faith and obedience; if man cannot recover the "blissful solitude" of Adam and Eve in the Garden, he can at least resist the lures of a corrupt society. The last two books of the poem demonstrate that the only true pastoral refuge, where one can find ease from passions and doubts and an assurance of harmony with God, is the soul. At the end of the true Christian's pilgrimage lies the secure paradise of heaven.

Each of the following chapters deals with some aspect of Milton's use of pastoral elements in his epic and traces this aspect throughout the poem. Rather than proceeding systematically from Book 1 to Book 12, I consider parts of *Paradise Lost* more than once, from different perspectives. Together, the various chapters constitute an approach to the poem from a particular point of view rather than a comprehensive reading.

# MILTON'S PASTORAL VISION

# I

# DIVINE PASTORAL

In one of several important articles on the pastoral mode, the late Renato Poggioli called attention to the contrast between the Christian imperative to self-sacrifice and faith and the bucolic invitation to withdraw from the world, at least in the imagination.[1] Certainly, the Christian sense of life as struggle and the pastoral vision of a life of self-indulgent ease could scarcely be more incompatible. Yet it does not necessarily follow that the contrast of city and country is alien to the Christian vision, as Poggioli goes on to argue. Poggioli cites the example of Dante, for whom Rome stood for civilization and the highest form of both secular and spiritual order. Needless to say, Protestants viewed the imperial city from a different historic and theological perspective. In fact, Puritans tended to regard all cities as evil and knew better than to look for any "continuing city" (Heb. 13:14) in this world.

Poggioli does consider some kinds of Christian pastoral, notably the pastoral elegies with a Christian

1. "The Oaten Flute," *Harvard Library Bulletin* 11 (1957): 147–84.

consolation (for example, *Lycidas),* reworkings of Virgil's messianic eclogue into hymns on the nativity of Christ, and allegorical uses of pastoral conventions to satirize corrupt clergy. But he concludes that "the critical mind can only treat as failures all attempts to Christianize the pastoral, or to translate Christianity into pastoral terms" (p. 236). Such a judgment on Christian uses of pastoral forms and conventions, whatever its merits, does not account for the kind of pastoral vision that Milton created in *Paradise Lost.* In epic tradition before *Paradise Lost,* particularly in Renaissance epic, pastoral episodes are usually interludes that slow or in some way deflect the course of the main action, as in Erminia's stay among the shepherds in *Jerusalem Delivered* or Calidore's comparable adventure in Book 6 of *The Faerie Queene.* The false paradises, or false pastoral retreats, of Tasso and Spenser constitute a more serious threat to heroic action. Their Circean enchantresses, far from living a simple, rustic life, pervert the natural world by bringing to it the refinements of court. Sensual pleasure is not so debilitating or reprehensible for Homer's Odysseus, though his sojourns with Circe and Calypso do delay his return home and his eventual vengeance on the suitors.

Aeneas's visit to the rural kingdom of Evander and his transplanted Arcadians in Book 8 of the *Aeneid* represents a different kind of pastoral episode, one that is closer to *Paradise Lost* in important ways. Pallanteum plays a crucial role in the epic, both as the future site of Rome and as a nucleus of moral values that Virgil saw as essential to the health of the Roman Empire. Aeneas must journey up the Tiber to get necessary military aid and to be schooled by Evander in frugality, humility, and piety (in the annual rites honoring Hercules, who serves as an example of martial valor). Both Virgil and Milton use values associated with pastoral life to test the traditional virtues of the epic hero, embodied by Turnus in the *Aeneid* and Satan in *Paradise Lost*, but the values that Adam absorbs are incompatible with militarism of any sort. Actually, Milton's pastoral vision could not be contained within the traditional historical framework of the epic. Virgil's perspective in Book 8 reaches back to the peace of the Golden Age under Saturn, associated with Pallanteum, and ahead to the pax Romana achieved under Augustus. But for Milton the temporal spectrum of human history is bounded by the timeless worlds of Eden and the heavenly paradise. The epic of man's spiritual struggle in the world belongs to a larger action that includes Satan's revolt and the creation of the world, and this action can be comprehended only from the perspective of God.

The divine plan for man's eventual salvation outlined by God in Book 3 explains why Eden assumes far greater importance in *Paradise Lost* than Pallanteum does in the *Aeneid*. Virgil was concerned with the destiny of Aeneas and the Roman Empire (his poem is dominated by a particular idea of history), Milton with illuminating the relationship of God and man. Thus in Milton's epic a pastoral vision of the initial stages of that relationship could legitimately claim more attention than the flow of history. Pallanteum is a stage in Aeneas's journey, a place where he can pause and orient himself politically and morally. Eden, as Milton envisioned it, is as much a state of being as a place. In Eden Adam and Eve are in a unique position to understand their relationship to God and to enjoy it, because there is no imperative to action, no reason to abandon the "uninterrupted joy" and "blissful solitude" that give them their extraordinary peacefulness.

We are not accustomed to thinking of Milton's Eden in the context of pastoral poetry because it is so obviously a special case, a prelapsarian world where there are no "busie companies of men" to flee. One of the best ways to see how the life of Adam and Eve is unique is to consider its relationship to commoner varieties of pastoral. How does Milton's pastoral vision differ from those we encounter in Renaissance lyrics, prose romances, and pastoral dramas? In the first place, Milton asks us to accept Eden with complete seriousness, as truth and not as a kind of literary balm for minds bruised by the contentions and deceits of court or city. Moreover, life in Eden before the arrival of Satan is remarkably uncomplicated, even for a pastoral world, because the source of all virtue is obedience.[2] Although Milton occasionally illustrates innocence for the reader in terms of its opposite ("the tedious pomp that waits / On Princes" [5. 354–55], "Court Amours, / Mixt Dance, or wanton Mask, or Midnight Ball" [4. 767–68]),[3] he did not need to justify pastoral life by dwelling on this contrast. Spenser's Melibeus must lecture Calidore on the differences between the court and the country, the misery of the rich and powerful and the happiness of the poor. But Adam inhabits a pristine world without geographical and social distinctions of the sort that Melibeus refers to

2. See Stanley Fish's appendix, "Notes on the Moral Unity of *Paradise Lost*," in *Surprised by Sin: The Reader in "Paradise Lost"* (New York, 1967). Fish discusses the sense in which all values are one in Eden, since they depend upon obedience.

3. Quotations of Milton's poetry are from the Columbia edition of *The Works of John Milton*, ed. Frank Allen Patterson (New York, 1931–42), hereafter cited as CE.

so self-consciously. The virtuous life is defined for him by God, not by his sense of the vices of a more sophisticated and corrupt world. He is secure because he knows his duties, the limitations of his knowledge, and what his happiness consists of.

Eden most resembles other versions of pastoral in offering the prospect of a harmonious and easy life. The charm of much pastoral poetry is that it presents a world in which friendship and love can flourish without the pressures imposed by ordinary life. Hostilities dissolve in a pervasive social harmony nurtured by a natural setting that delights the senses and removes the necessity for hard labor. The essential tranquillity of such an imagined world can be seen in a typical lyric from *England's Helicon,* which recreates the Golden Age in the language of Elizabethan pastoral:

> *Fields were over-spread with flowers,*
> *Fairest choise of* Floraes *treasure:*
> *Sheepheards there had shadie Bowers,*
> *Where they oft reposed with pleasure.*
> *Meadowes flourish'd fresh and gay,*
> *where the wanton Heards did play.*
>
> *Springs more cleare then Christall streames,*
> *Seated were the Groves among:*
> *Thus nor* Titans *scorching beames,*
> *Nor earths drouth could Sheepheards wrong.*
> *Faire* Pomonaes *fruitfull pride:*
> *did the budding braunches hide.*
>
> *Flocks of sheepe fed on the Plaines,*
> *Harmelesse sheepe that roamd at large:*
> *Heere and there sate pensive Swaines,*
> *Wayting on their wandring charge.*

*Pensive while their Lasses smil'd:*
*Lasses which had them beguil'd.*

*Hills with trees were richly dight,*
*Vallies stor'd with* Vestaes *wealth:*
*Both did harbour sweet delight,*
*Nought was there to hinder health.*
*Thus did heaven grace the soyle:*
*Not deform'd with work-mens toile.*[4]

The scene could almost be Eden, if one imagined Adam and Eve in the place of shepherds and their lasses, except that the most important element of Milton's pastoral is lacking: a sense of the divine presence.

Nature in Eden leads the mind and the affections to God. Adam's conversation continually reminds the reader that God is the author of paradise and the ultimate source of human happiness; he even speaks of sleep, the most ordinary of human activities, as a "gift" from God. Adam never forgets that Eden is the "Gard'n of God," although Eve sometimes appears to. Ironically, the one passage that could be detached from the poem and anthologized as a pastoral lyric is given to Eve. Her lovely tribute to Adam, "With thee conversing I forget all time" (4. 639–56), is a statement of personal devotion, a self-contained expression of delight that circles back upon itself. One does not need a reference point outside of Eden in order to appreciate it.

Most visions of pastoral life offer freedom from the distractions that consume our energies and make real tranquillity impossible, appealing to our feeling that if

4. From *England's Helicon*, ed. Hugh Macdonald (Cambridge, Mass., 1962), pp. 33–34. The author is known only by his initials, J. M. I have omitted the last stanza.

life were only simple enough we could be "whole again beyond confusion," to borrow a haunting phrase from Frost's "Directive." Milton tried to present a true vision of a time before confusion had been introduced into human life. In the process he enlarged the scope of pastoral by making bliss dependent upon man's consciousness of the larger harmony of all creation with God. We can take the contentment of the "pensive" shepherds of the lyric for granted. Adam's depends upon a capacity for understanding the conditions of his innocence. This understanding deepens as he learns from Raphael

> *to know*
> *That which before us lies in daily life*
> *Is the prime Wisdom.*
>
> (8. 192–94)

Adam can satisfy himself with being "lowly wise" because everything that he encounters in his daily life declares God's goodness "beyond thought" (5. 159). Heaven, Raphael tells him, is set before man as the "Book of God . . . Wherein to read his wond'rous Works" (8. 67–68). Aided by his celestial tutor, Adam learns to recognize the "scale of Nature":

> *Whereon*
> *In contemplation of created things*
> *By steps we may ascend to God.*
>
> (5. 510–12)

One is struck by the ease with which Adam can see the goodness and order of his world before he falls into the condition of having to know good by evil, like Psyche laboriously sorting her seeds.[5] Such privileged knowledge

5. See *Areopagitica,* CE, 4:310.

hangs by the thread of obedience, of course. Once Adam has sinned, his eyes are covered by a "Film" which Michael must dissolve in order to reveal to him man's future.

Milton's conception of the innocent Adam's vision of truth is fundamentally Platonic. Adapting Plato's parable of the cave, one might say that Adam and Eve in their original condition have not yet entered the cave but wander about in a bright upper world, intuitively recognizing God as the source of all goodness. Although they cannot approach the "Fountain of Light" (3. 375) itself in their human state, the sun that each morning "spreads / His orient Beams, on herb, tree, fruit, and flour" (4. 543–44) continually reminds them of the Creator and seems to unify their world. In Eden the sun can serve as it did for Ficino, as a symbol of God (Satan imagines the sun as looking from its "sole Dominion like the God / Of this new World" [4. 33–34]). In Ficino's conception light connects the celestial and the earthly; it is "the bond of the universe."[6] Light in Eden functions in much the same way.

Their perception unclouded by sin, Adam and Eve can appreciate the unity of the natural world and its harmony with heaven. In the morning hymn of Book 5 they see all movement as patterned celebration: "let your ceaseless change / Varie to our great Maker still new praise" (5. 183–84). Milton associated this kind of perception, and the possibility of a neo-Platonic ascent to

6. In *De lumine, Opera omnia* (Basel, 1561), p. 981, as translated by Paul Oskar Kristeller in *The Philosophy of Marsilio Ficino* (New York, 1943), p. 116. I am indebted to Frank Huntley's recent discussion of Platonism in *Paradise Lost,* "Before and After the Fall: Some Miltonic Patterns of Systasis," in *Approaches to "Paradise Lost,"* ed. C. A. Patrides (London, 1968), pp. 1–14.

God (through "contemplation of created things"), exclusively with the condition of innocence. Fallen man must think historically, in terms of God's intervention in the long chain of events precipitated by the first sinful act to redeem mankind and renew the corrupted earth.

Even the gardening labor of Adam and Eve reinforces their awareness of God. This delightful activity, which distinguishes them from the more sedentary shepherds of pastoral tradition, structures their daily lives and secures their place in the scale of nature:

> *Man hath his daily work of body or mind*
> *Appointed, which declares his Dignitie,*
> *And the regard of Heav'n on all his waies;*
> *While other Animals unactive range,*
> *And of thir doings God takes no account.*
> (4. 618–22)

Adam's work not only assures him that he enjoys the "regard of Heav'n," it heightens his appreciation of the miraculous fertility of the Garden.

The hexaemeral writers understood better than we are likely to that the foundation of Adam's bliss was his sense of the closeness of God. Du Bartas put it plainly:

> *But, Adam's best and supreme delectation*
> *Was th'often haunt and holy conversation*
> *His soule and body had so many wayes*
> *With God; who lightened* Eden *with his Rayes.*[7]

Milton found effective ways of dramatizing this immediacy. When critics of *Paradise Lost* speak of the harshness of Milton's God, they are referring to God the Father

7. *The Complete Works of Joshua Sylvester,* ed. A. B. Grosart (Edinburg, 1880), 1:102.

as he appears in heavenly discourses with the Son. Seen as the upholder of divine justice, as it applies to man and to Satan, God is indeed an austere and remote figure. Yet when Milton describes Eden, God appears in a different aspect, as the "Universal Lord" who "fram'd / All things to man's delightful use" (4. 691–92). C. A. Patrides has argued convincingly that Milton avoided distinguishing between Father and Son outside of heaven. According to Patrides, the "Presence Divine" of Book 8 should be regarded as "God addressing Adam in the unity of the Godhead."[8] We see God in this initial encounter with man not as Father or Son but as the benevolent and paternal Author of the universe, the "Creator bounteous and benign" (8. 492). For the moment we forget the "Almighty Power" of Book 3 and experience God as Adam does. The "gratious voice Divine" becomes stern only once, in warning Adam of the consequences of disobeying the "sole Command."

Milton took great care to make God appear "gracious" in Book 8, even to the point of introducing humor into the dialogue of God and man. In the economical narrative of Genesis Yahweh only commands, and man does not enjoy the privilege of conversation. The most remarkable thing about Milton's version of the scene is that Adam can talk with God so easily. His simple, candid responses show that originally divinity did not terrify or intimidate man, even though the effort of participating in "celestial Colloquy sublime" might exhaust him.

Adam's retrospective view of what he has lost affords the best indication in the poem of Milton's view of man's original relationship with God:

8. "The Godhead in *Paradise Lost:* Dogma or Drama?" *Journal of English and Germanic Philology* 64 (1965):29–34.

*This most afflicts me, that departing hence,*
*As from his face I shall be hid, depriv'd*
*His blessed count'nance; here I could frequent,*
*With worship, place by place where he voutsaf'd*
*Presence Divine, and to my Sons relate;*
*On this Mount he appear'd, under this Tree*
*Stood visible, among these Pines his voice*
*I heard, here with him at this Fountain talk'd.*
(11. 316–22)

As Louis Martz has shown, this sense of the closeness of God suggests Vaughan's meditations on the "white days" of the patriarchs and Traherne's attempts in prose and poetry to imagine the state of Adam.[9] Yet Martz's interesting comparisons obscure an essential difference between the movement of Milton's epic and the meditative quests of Vaughan and Traherne. Their emphasis is on the individual's recovery of communion with God, whereas Milton's, in the last two books of *Paradise Lost* at least, is on the adjustments that the Fall necessitates in man's ways of apprehending God.

Part of Michael's task is to show Adam how to make these adjustments. He counters the literalism of Adam's troubled question, "In yonder nether World where shall I seek / His bright appearances, or footsteps trace?" (11. 328–29), with the assurance that God's "Omnipresence" fills the earth:

*Yet doubt not but in Valley and in Plain*
*God is as here, and will be found alike*
*Present, and of his presence many a sign*
*Still following thee, still compassing thee round*

9. In *The Paradise Within* (New Haven, 1964).

*With goodness and paternal Love, his Face*
*Express, and of his steps the track Divine.*
(11. 349–54)

With this consoling explanation Michael throws into sharp relief two different modes of knowing God. We are educated with Adam in the ways in which fallen man can be conscious of the divine presence. Adam in his innocence could see God face to face; now he must learn to rely on signs and to anticipate the time when he will look on the face of God in heaven. After walking with God, he must learn what it is "to walk / As in his presence" (12. 562–63). Michael's instruction is in part a lesson in how to think metaphorically, the sort of lesson that Richard Baxter gave his readers at more length in his treatise *Walking with God,* drawing out the practical applications of the metaphor.[10]

The historical pageant that Michael presents effectively illustrates the changed relationship of God and man, or rather the vicissitudes of that relationship. Book 11 is a study in human corruption and man's progressive alienation from God, an alienation that leads to a terrible visitation of divine wrath in the form of the flood. God's covenant with Noah, signified by the rainbow, is followed by the moral deterioration of Noah's descendants, until God again withdraws his presence and averts "His holy Eyes" (12. 109). God leads the Israelites out of Egypt, establishing his presence through the cloud and pillar of fire that guide them, and sets up his tabernacle among them, "The Holy One with mortal Men to dwell" (12. 248), but then responds to "foul Idolatries" by abandoning them before the power of Babylon. These cycles,

10. In *The Divine Life in Three Treatises* (London, 1664).

which illustrate the strength of the "sinfulness of Men" with which "supernal Grace" must contend, prepare Adam to rejoice at being told of the Nativity and the prospect of Christ's eventual reign. They also insure that his renewed love for God will be tempered with fear ("Henceforth I learn, that to obey is best, / And love with fear the only God" [12. 561–62]).

Martz complains that the "strict equation of earth with evil" in Book 11 produces a feeling that "nothing much has been accomplished by Milton's beautiful demonstration that the vision of Paradise can be recovered by the mind of man, fallen and redeemed."[11] But this criticism assumes that Milton's purpose in writing *Paradise Lost* was to show how we can recover such a vision. Was it not rather to make us recognize, by contrasting it with Eden, that our world is a wilderness through which we must wander with the aid of faith and a reliance upon providence? Traherne was able to say that, if you love God, "the World shall be a Grand Jewel of Delight unto you: a very Paradice; and the Gate of Heaven."[12] In the last two books of *Paradise Lost* Milton deliberately moved in the opposite direction, dramatizing the gulf between the fallen world and paradise. This strategy has the effect of directing the reader's attention from earth to heaven, the "eternal Paradise of rest" (12. 314) that man will eventually gain. From Michael's apocalyptic per-

11. *The Paradise Within*, p. 154.

12. *Thomas Traherne: Centuries, Poems, and Thanksgivings*, ed. H. M. Margoliouth (Oxford, 1958), 1:10. See also ibid., p. 14: "Your Enjoyment of the World is never right, till evry Morning you awake in Heaven: see your self in your fathers Palace: and look upon the Skies and the Earth and the Air, as Celestial Joys: having such a Reverend Esteem of all, as if you were among the Angels."

spective the entire earth appears as a part of Satan's empire. It is "*his* perverted World," which must be dissolved before Christ can raise new heavens and earth, "purg'd and refin'd" (12. 548).

Michael's promise of a "paradise within" may seem to contradict this line of argument, but seen in context the phrase does not suggest anything like the inner paradise that Traherne created for himself by meditation. Throughout the latter part of his dialogue with Adam Michael emphasizes the ways in which God will help us to live in the world. He will send men a Comforter "who shall dwell / His Spirit within them" (12. 487–88) and arm them with spiritual armor "able to resist / *Satan's* assaults, and quench his fiery darts" (12. 491–92). The faithful will be able to amaze their "proudest persecutors" by withstanding them to the point of martyrdom. The sense of a "paradise within" is to be attained not by meditation but through the exercise of faith, virtue, patience, temperance, and love; and it reflects the inner strength and "peace / Of Conscience" (12. 296–97) that assurance of salvation can give. Such a state of mind is "happier" than man's original bliss, since it includes an awareness of what unhappiness is. The redeemed can take more satisfaction than the innocent Adam in obedience to God because obedience is so much more difficult in the fallen world. And their suffering enables them to take greater joy in the prospect of celestial bliss.

On two occasions, in Book 3 (530–34) and again in Book 7 (569–73), Milton refers obliquely to those divine visitations described in the Old Testament that so affected Vaughan, but the chief impression of life in the fallen world given by Books 11 and 12 is of God's remoteness. The one appearance of God on earth that Milton records is his descent to Sinai, and this occasion provides a striking contrast with the conversation of God and Adam in Book 8. Milton's account, like that of Genesis, stresses the power and dreadfulness of God:

> *God from the Mount of* Sinai, *whose gray top*
> *Shall tremble, he descending, will himself*
> *In Thunder, Lightning and loud Trumpet's sound*
> *Ordain them Laws.*
>
> (12. 227–30)

Milton omitted the conversation of God with Moses preceding the confrontation, instead emphasizing the fear of the people ("the voice of God / To mortal ear is dreadful") and the necessity of approaching God through a mediator. A sense of man's inadequacy before the divine presence underlies the scene, as well as the last three books of the poem. The distinction that Milton insisted upon is essentially the one made by the Puritan theologian, William Perkins, half a century earlier:

> [The] fellowship betweene God and man in his innocencie, was made manifest in the familiar conference which God vouchsafed to man: but since the fall this communion is lost, for man cannot abide the presence of God.[13]

Adam's outcry upon recognizing his guilt is a dramatic equivalent for Perkins' statement:

> *How shall I behold the face*
> *Henceforth of God or Angel, erst with joy*
> *And rapture so oft beheld? those heav'nly shapes*
> *Will dazzle now this earthly, with thir blaze*
> *Insufferably bright.*
>
> (9. 1080–84)

13. *Works* (London, 1612), p. 151.

Economy is not the only explanation for the notable omissions in Milton's historical narrative. To have included events such as Abraham's attempted sacrifice of Isaac or Jacob's dream would have called attention to a contact between human and divine that Milton was trying to deemphasize. The contrast between his use of the Old Testament and Traherne's is revealing. Traherne, meditating on Genesis, was not concerned with distinguishing between Adam's experience and that of the patriarchs:

> There I saw Jacob, with Awful Apprehensions Admiring the Glory of the World, when awaking out of His Dream he said, How dreadfull is this Place? This is none other then the Hous of GOD, and the Gate of Heaven. There I saw God leading forth Abraham, and shewing him the Stars of Heaven; and all the Countries round about him, and saying All these I will give Thee, and thy Seed after Thee. There I saw Adam in Paradice, surrounded by the Beauty of Heaven and Earth.[14]

Significantly, Milton refers to Jacob's ladder in Book 3 rather than in Book 12.[15] The golden stairs seen by Satan serve as striking evidence of the communication between heaven and earth before the Fall (the passage of heaven

14. *Traherne,* 1:149.

15. See George Wesley Whiting, *Milton and This Pendant World* (Austin, Texas, 1958), chap. 3, for a discussion of exegetical commentary on Jacob's ladder. Whiting shows that in Protestant tradition the ladder was generally identified with Christ, seen as mediator and redeemer, though it was sometimes used to symbolize steps to the perfection of spiritual life. See also C. A. Patrides, *Milton and the Christian Tradition* (Oxford, 1966), p. 227.

to earth is "Wider by far than that of after times / Over Mount *Sion*" [3. 529–30]); the contrasting symbol is the bridge of Sin and Death which consolidates Satan's empire, enlarged by the conquest of the earth.

Theologically, the instances of man's alienation from God are nullified by the prospect of the incarnation ("So God with man unites" [12. 382]) and man's eventual union with God in heaven. And Adam's sorrow is in effect nullified by the joy that leads him to exclaim, "O Goodness infinite, goodness immense!" (11. 469). But the extreme attention to human sinfulness which Martz finds disproportionate ("in poetry, can a hundred lines of hopeful doctrine outweigh six hundred lines of visionary woe?") is necessary if the reader is to be convinced, with Adam, to put his trust in a heavenly rather than an earthly kingdom. He must recognize fully the capacity of human society for violence and corruption if he is to regard life as a constant state of spiritual warfare which affords no rest, not even the rest that is the final state of the mystic's spiritual journey to God, until he finally enters the "Holy Rest" of God. The interaction of visions of communion and visions of alienation, evocations of paradisal bliss and of truth retiring "Bestuck with sland'rous darts" (12. 536), arises from the dynamics of the poem, as the contrast between the persecutions of the saints and the bliss of their "seasonable rest" arises from the dynamics of Richard Baxter's theology:

> When we have endured a hard winter in this cold Climate, will not the reviving spring be then seasonable? . . . When we have had a long and perilous War, and have lived in the midst of furious Enemies, and have been forced to stand on a perpetual watch, and received from

> them many a wound; would not a peace with victory be to us seasonable? . . . Will not *Canaan* be seasonable after so many years travel, and that through a hazardous and grievous Wilderness?[16]

The apocalyptic prophecies of both men owe their intensity to a bitter consciousness of the uncertainty and pain of the journey.

Milton's treatment of Adam's original communion with God takes on a new richness when one returns to it from a reading of the last two books. With the promise of redemption in mind, one can regard Eden as a foreshadowing of the joys of heaven. The presence of "Millions of spiritual Creatures" (4. 677) who walk the earth unseen and raise their "Celestial voices" in nightly songs of praise makes Eden seem virtually an outlying province of heaven. These "millions" serve as a reminder of the nearness of God and the dependence of all things upon him; as Adam says, they "lift our thoughts to heaven." Earlier in Book 4 Milton establishes the protective presence of Gabriel and his angelic guards. The social presence of the angels is symbolized by the visit of Raphael, an occasion which we are led to regard as typical of life in Eden:

> *No more of talk where God or Angel Guest*
> *With Man, as with his Friend, familiar us'd*
> *To sit indulgent, and with him partake*
> *Rural repast, permitting him the while*
> *Venial discourse unblam'd.*
>
> (9. 1–5)

16. *The Saints Everlasting Rest* (London, 1649), pp. 92–93.

There were no real precedents in epic tradition for the kind of relationship that Milton illustrated by Raphael's visit. When celestial messengers descend to earth to prophesy or instruct, they do not stay for dinner.[17] The fact that Raphael does, and that Adam and Eve entertain him with consummate social poise, indicates that Milton wanted to call special attention to the easy rapport between man and angel before the Fall. Their social interaction underscores the continuity of all states of being and makes more plausible Raphael's suggestion that men may come to eat with the angels when they "turn all to spirit" (5. 497). The brief indication that Raphael gives of the "communion sweet" of the angels in their heavenly feasting, like all the other indications of life in heaven, is extremely important in establishing a broader context in which Adam can view his daily life. With admirable tact Raphael praises the delicacies of Eden and at the same time makes Adam realize that the highest bliss is to "quaff immortality and joy" in the actual presence of "th'all bounteous King" (5. 640). Adam should experience the sensuous pleasures of dining on "fruit of all kinds," since Raphael enjoins him to enjoy "Your fill what happiness this happy state / Can comprehend, incapable of more" (5. 504–5). But he must recognize that there is more, and his recognition points the reader also to heaven.

Some critics have called the meal in Eden sacramental, but the word suggests a self-conscious celebration of a

17. There are analogues for Milton's emphasis on the familiarity of man with the angels in hexaemeral literature. In Andreini's *L'Adamo* the angels weave garlands of flowers for Adam and Eve. In Vondel's *Adam in Ballingschap* they prepare a wedding feast.

holy mystery in the attempt to achieve communion with God.[18] William Perkins defined a sacrament as that "whereby Christ and his saving graces are by certaine externall rites, signified, exhibited, and sealed to a Christian man."[19] Participating in the Lord's Supper implies "a sacramental relation of sensible and externall actions and spiritual and internal actions." The necessity for symbolically joining the life of the senses and that of the spirit simply does not exist in Eden, because there is no division between the external and the internal man before the Fall. Every action of Adam's—eating, laboring, even lovemaking—is an implicit affirmation of his love of God and dependence upon him. This wholeness of being is possible because Adam is conscious of how his life in paradise is a part of the natural order established by God, of how it in fact pleases God. As we see from his comments to Raphael about the attraction of Eve's beauty, Adam cannot always let his pleasure be his guide. But he is quick to respond to correction and, in his innocence, is entirely submissive to what he understands to be the will of God.

18. More recently, John M. Steadman (in *Milton's Epic Characters* [Chapel Hill, 1968], p. 89) has cited Milton's statement in *Christian Doctrine* that the tree of life ought not to be considered so much a sacrament as a symbol of eternal life, and Anthony Low (in "Angels and Food in *Paradise Lost,*" *Milton Studies,* 1 [Pittsburgh, 1969]:135–44) has argued that the scene reflects "the Protestant or Puritan Communion Service," which Milton did not regard as a sacrament but a "solemnity." Low sees the meal as "a central symbol of the prelapsarian life," "signifying the communion between Angel and Man, between Heaven and Earth, and between Man and God" (p. 144).

19. *Works* (London, 1612), p. 71. In *Christian Doctrine,* CE, 16:201, Milton defines a sacrament as "a seal of the covenant of grace."

The meal shared with Raphael invites comparison with the "Heavenly Feast" of the triumphant Son at the end of *Paradise Regained:*[20]

> *Then in a flow'ry valley [the angels] set him down*
> *On a green bank, and set before him spread.*
> *A table of Celestial Food, Divine,*
> *Ambrosial, Fruits fetcht from the tree of life,*
> *And from the fount of life Ambrosial drink.*
> (4. 586–90)

This feast obviously surpasses the one in Eden in symbolic value; the food is not from earth but heaven, and it commemorates a highly significant victory. But the very fact that the meal of Adam and Raphael is so natural, something that might almost be an everyday occurrence in paradise, makes the comparison interesting. Jesus's great weariness, emphasized by his dependence on the offices of angels who transport him to the "flow'ry valley," suggests the extreme difficulty of recovering what Adam and Eve so easily lost. Even the valley takes the mind back to Eden and the more luxuriant natural setting that Adam and Eve enjoy. All meals there, except the fatal act of eating the fruit of the Tree of Knowledge, embody the divine promise of immortal life. And, as Adam's invitation to Raphael demonstrates, they also involve an awareness of the immensity of man's indebtedness to God:

> *Heav'nly Stranger, please to taste*
> *These bounties which our Nourisher, from whom*

20. John M. Steadman has described this event as a symbol of the recovery of paradise for mankind and of Christ's redemptive mission. *Milton's Epic Characters,* pp. 82–89.

*All perfet good unmeasur'd out, descends,*
*To us for food and for delight hath caus'd*
*The Earth to yield.*

(5. 397–401)

Of all the scenes in Eden the dinner with Raphael is closest to the epic manner. It is a pastoral episode elevated to the seriousness and dignity of epic; consider the brilliance of Raphael's "state" and the solemnity of Adam's.[21] Milton could count on his more literate readers to see in the scene in Eden the admirable simplicity of other rural repasts—the meal of Calidore with Melibeus, or the more elaborate feast of Aeneas and Evander—and something else besides. His subject allowed him to be more serious about pastoral than his sage and serious teacher, and less self-conscious about the use of it. Instead of attempting to imitate rustic life, he could present the majesty of true primitivism. The ease of Adam and Eve in the presence of Raphael implies the "sweet peace" that Melibeus describes to Calidore and moves beyond it to a holy joy in the presence of an archangel.

Adam's sense of the sanctity of life distinguishes him from the inhabitants of other pastoral worlds. Eden appears as a vast natural temple where the flowers breathe

21. Both James H. Sims (*The Bible in Milton's Epics* [Gainesville, Florida, 1962], pp. 202–205) and Harold Fisch ("Hebraic Style and Motifs in *Paradise Lost,*" in *Language and Style in Milton,* ed. R. D. Emma and John T. Shawcross [New York, 1967], pp. 53–54) see in the scene the biblical realism of Abraham's encounter with his angelic visitors (Gen. 18). I have tried to show elsewhere that the presentation of Adam and Eve here is not at all realistic in this sense but much closer to the blend of majesty and simplicity that Virgil achieved in describing Evander. See my article, "The Visit of Raphael: *Paradise Lost,* Book 5," *Philological Quarter* 47 (1968):75–85.

"morning incense," sending up "silent praise" to the Creator from "th' Earth's great altar" (9. 195), and Adam and Eve instinctively greet each new day with a hymn. It is significant that the hymn Milton presents in Book 5 (153–208) serves as the means by which Adam and Eve recover "firm peace" and "wonted calm" after Eve's disturbing dream. The very capacity to offer spontaneous and eloquent praise, in "various style," is a reminder of their special relationship with God.[22] To read the hymn is to recognize that fallen man has lost the intuitive sense of what constitutes "fit" praise and is far from being able to offer it without meditation. By comparison, the penitential prayer with which Book 10 closes indicates how far man has fallen. The morning hymn is obviously much closer to angelic songs of celebration than to this indirectly described confession of guilt. In their abjectness Adam and Eve seem to have lost all confidence in their own dignity and in God's protective love. Their prayer is answered, of course, but by stressing Christ's mediatorial role Milton makes the reader aware of the distance between man and God.

Milton suggests an even sharper contrast between the "holy rapture" of the innocent Adam and Eve and the worship of those who "will deem in outward Rites and specious forms / Religion satisfied" (12. 534–35). This rebuke of sterile formalism recalls Milton's more passionate denunciation of the "sensual idolatry" of Catholicism in *Of Reformation in England:*

> They began to draw down all the divine intercourse betwixt God and the soul, yea, the very

22. See Joseph H. Summers's excellent analysis of the hymn itself, *The Muse's Method* (Cambridge, Mass., 1962), pp. 75–85.

> shape of God himself, into an exterior and bodily form, urgently pretending a necessity and obligement of joining the body in a formal reverence and worship circumscribed . . . till the soul by this means of overbodying herself, given up justly to fleshly delights, bated her wing apace downward: and finding the ease she had from her visible and sensuous colleague, the body, in performance of religious duties, her pinions now broken and flagging, shifted off from herself the labour of high soaring any more, forgot her heavenly flight, and left the dull and droiling carcass to plod on in the old road and drudging trade of outward conformity.[23]

The point of Milton's argument here is to show that faith does not need the "weak and fallible offices of the senses." The hymn in Eden illustrates a properly spiritual mode of worship, a higher form of "divine intercourse of the soul and God" than fallen man can achieve, and points to the highest form of this intercourse, the continuous praise of the angels who circle the throne of God rejoicing. Adam and Eve in their innocence can trust their senses. Indeed, the richness of the hymn depends upon their sensuous apprehension of the texture and rhythms of their natural world: mists colored by the sun, trees waving their tops in the wind, streams "warbling" their praise. The congruence of sensuous and spiritual response is another evidence of the wholeness of man's nature before the Fall.

More fully than anything else in the poem the hymn

23. CE, 3:pt. 1:2–3.

reveals a unified natural world with which man is completely in tune. A similar feeling of harmony and assurance pervades the hymn to Pan near the end of Fletcher's *The Faithful Shepherdess*[24]—a celebration of a simple, pastoral world presided over by a benevolent deity—but Milton's more comprehensive vision of order extends to the "mystic Dance" of the planets and the circling of the angels about God. Fletcher creates an illusion of harmony between man and nature by having the "virtues" and "powers" of the natural world dance to the songs of shepherds and shepherdesses in praise of Pan. Milton's pastoral world, however, is neither self-sufficient nor self-delighting. To be attuned to nature in Eden is to be attuned to God, for the rhythm to which Adam and Eve respond is established by God and continuously glorifies him. Most visions of a delightful pastoral world are complete in themselves, but the dynamism of Milton's paradise forces one to recognize the source of all movement, and its end.

The encounters with the Son and with Michael that follow the Fall demonstrate the breach between human

24. Here is the first of two stanzas:

*All ye woods, and trees, and bowers,*
*All ye virtues and ye powers*
*That inhabit in the lakes,*
*In the pleasant springs or brakes,*
*Move your feet*
*To the sound,*
*Whilst we greet*
*All this ground*
*With his honour and his name*
*That defends our flock from blame.*

In *Beaumont and Fletcher's Plays,* ed. G. P. Baker, Everyman edition (London, 1911), p. 312.

and divine opened by man's sin. Milton eased the shock by making the Son combine the roles of mediator and judge, tempering justice with the implicit promise of mercy, and by having Michael console Adam before banishing him from Eden. Yet Michael remains a severe figure who will not acknowledge Adam's bow or sit down with him.[25] Milton emphasized Michael's military posture. He is a commander whose charge is to expel now "tainted" man and prevent access to the Tree of Life; his first act upon arriving in Eden is to dispatch "his Powers to seize / Possession of the Garden" (11. 221–22). With the occupation Eden effectively becomes a garrison.

Michael's military role is significant in another respect. Part of his task is to prepare Adam for the transition from a pastoral existence to what can be called an epic mode of life. The "Puritan epic of spiritual life," to use William Haller's phrase,[26] begins with the Fall, and Michael, the supreme military figure among the angels, is well suited to describe to Adam God's spiritual armor and man's future combat with Satan in the world. Michael does not exemplify the new kind of heroism he describes to Adam, a Christian heroism based on patience, but then the battles on the plains of heaven are not the sort that Adam will have to fight. Michael acts as an agent of divine power, sent to convince man that God's providence will bring about a final victory over evil. Adam himself must learn to rely on faith rather than strength, "by things deem'd weak / Subverting worldly strong" (12. 567–68).

25. Low comments on the contrast between Michael and Raphael in "Angels and Food in *Paradise Lost,*" pp. 143–44.

26. In *The Rise of Puritanism* (New York, 1938).

When Adam leaves the Garden, he moves from a pastoral life of contemplation, nurtured by visits such as Raphael's, into a life of active labor and spiritual struggle. As a wayfaring Christian journeying through the world, Adam will be comforted and strengthened by evidences of God's presence. Having left the natural temple of the Garden, he will himself become "the temple of the living God."[27] If Milton's discussion of the state of the redeemed in *Christian Doctrine* can be regarded as applying to Adam, and surely it can, he will share in the union and fellowship with the Father through the Son which is possible to the regenerate.[28] We can assume that in the state of imperfect glorification Adam will be filled with a consciousness of present grace and an expectation of future glory.[29] Yet Milton's emphasis in *Paradise Lost* is not on imperfect but perfect glorification, not on the invisible church of the saved but on the final union of Adam and all the faithful who follow him with God. The angelic songs of rejoicing anticipate the time when "God shall be All in All" (3. 341).

In *Paradise Lost* the image of perfect union with God complements and in a sense completes the various forms of communion with God in Eden. In man's progress through time, as Milton conceived it, there is nothing remotely comparable to his relationship to God in paradise or the final union to be enjoyed in heaven. The flaming sword that blocks the way back to the Garden symbolizes the impossibility of recovering in the world

27. 2 Corinthians, 6:16, quoted by Milton in *Christian Doctrine*. See CE, 16:61.

28. See CE, 16, chaps. 24 and 25.

29. CE, 16:66–67.

the state of mind associated with paradise.[30] This conception of experience in the fallen world is completely contrary to the mystic's sense of finding a garden, or paradise, within the soul. St. Teresa wrote, "it used to give me great delight to think of my soul as a garden and of the Lord as walking in it. I would beg Him to increase the fragrance of the little buds of virtue."[31] For St. Teresa and many others the most suggestive biblical garden was not paradise but the *hortus conclusus* of the Song of Songs, widely interpreted as an allegory of the marriage of Christ and the soul, or the church. Like St. Teresa, Vaughan found the Song of Songs a rich source of imagery in which to describe spiritual growth. His poem "Regeneration" charts a pilgrimage of the soul that ends in an enclosed garden where his soul experiences a new spring.

30. The end of learning, as Milton described it in *Of Education* (CE, 4:277) is "to repair the ruines of our first parents by regaining to know God aright." But to know God aright is not to know God with the sense of immediacy and joy that Adam experienced. It should be said that Milton never allows Adam any rapture that could be called mystical. Compare Vondel's conception of Adam's experience:

*Stand we in Eden, or among the stars?*
*What heavenly yearning ravishes my soul?*
*My feet can feel no earth: it sinks away.*
*The godlike sound of holy bridal song*
*Unties the bond that couples soul with body.*
*The soul, intent upon its heavenly nature,*
*Rejects the earthly and becomes a flame*
*That seeks the high, first source of its own being.*

*Adam in Ballingschap,* as translated by Watson Kirkconnell, *The Celestial Cycle* (Toronto, 1952), p. 459.

31. As quoted by Stanley Stewart in *The Enclosed Garden* (Madison, Wis., 1966), p. 109. See Stewart's very full discussion of the use of imagery from the Song of Songs, especially pp. 97–149.

In the Puritan conception of life as a pilgrimage—a linear, historical journey and not a journey of the mind to God—the faithful do not feel a "reviving spring," to use Baxter's phrase, until they reach the heavenly Canaan. The best illustration of the pattern is Bunyan's Christian, who experiences a foretaste of celestial bliss in the meadows and streams of Beulah as he nears the end of his journey. It is at this point that Bunyan drew upon the pastoral imagery of the Song of Songs. In his commentary on Revelation, *The Holy City,* Bunyan also associated the Song of Songs with heaven. For him the Tree of Life signified that the inhabitants of the heavenly city "shall be sweetly shadowed, refreshed, and defended, with its coolness, and also sweetly refreshed and comforted with its dainties."[32] The Puritan sense of the world as wilderness, which Milton shared, dictated that the spiritual rewards of paradise be found only at the end of the journey. Only there can the soul truly flower:

> Oh, they shall be green, savoury, reviving, flourishing, growing Christians that shall walk the street of New Jerusalem.[33]

32. *The Entire Works of John Bunyan,* ed. Henry Stebbing (London, 1859), 1:326. Bunyan quotes the Song of Solomon (2:3): "I sat down under his shadow with great delight, and his fruit was sweet to my taste."

33. Ibid.

# 2

# EDEN

IN 1753 JOSEPH WARTON, OBVIOUSLY NOT A MAN TO ECHO received opinion, said exactly what he thought of Milton's Eden:

> Sapphire fountains that rolling over orient pearl run nectar, roses without thorns, trees that bear fruit of vegetable gold and that weep odorous gums and balms are easily feigned, but having no relative beauty as pictures of nature, nor any absolute excellence as derived from truth, they can only please those who when they read exercise no faculty but fancy and admire because they do not think.[1]

The objections of such modern critics of Milton's stylized natural description as T. S. Eliot and F. R. Leavis are not so very different from Warton's in tone and bias.[2] The preference for realistic and detailed "pictures of nature"

1. Adventurer, 101. Quoted in *Eighteenth-Century Critical Essays,* ed. Elledge (Ithaca, N.Y., 1961), 2:713.

2. See T. S. Eliot, "A Note on the Verse of John Milton," *Essays and Studies,* 21 (1936):32–40, and F. R. Leavis, *Revaluation* (London, 1936), p. 47.

that Warton helped to establish and we take for granted makes it understandably difficult for a modern reader to appreciate the conventional modes of representing the earthly paradise, and for that matter any natural scene, that Milton inherited. But the important question to ask in responding to *Paradise Lost* is what kind of "truth" we should be seeking. Should paradise be sharply particularized, so that it appears as a recognizable, precisely defined place? Or should it represent a kind of imaginative truth by imaging a state of innocence and bliss beyond normal human experience? C. S. Lewis, a persuasive defender of Milton's conception of Eden, has argued that it had to be conventional, "immemorial" rather than original, to make us know that "the garden is found."[3] A narrow literalism would have defeated Milton's purpose of exposing the reader to a condition of life that is more nearly mythic than historic. He knew that we must shake off our bondage to the familiar, and temporarily forget our normal sense of time, if we are to respond fully to a prelapsarian world.

Even though poets might all agree that spring was eternal here and the fruit golden, they found different ways of appealing to "fancy" in describing the earthly paradise. Milton's Eden is not to be compared with those medieval versions of paradise that have richly jewelled gates, or palaces, or fountains. Actually Milton's "Saphire Fount," "Orient Pearl," and "sands of Gold" need not

3. *A Preface to Paradise Lost* (London, 1942), p. 51. See also Douglas Bush's similar defense, *"Paradise Lost" in Our Time* (Ithaca, N.Y., 1945), and J. B. Broadbent's commentary on Milton's paradise in *Some Graver Subject* (New York, 1960) 173–84. The fullest and best treatment of the earthly paradise tradition is A. Bartlett Giamatti's *The Earthly Paradise and The Renaissance Epic* (Princeton, 1966).

be taken as literally as Warton supposes. One can find similar diction in *Comus,* where Sabrina's "silver lake" and "coral-pav'n bed," and her chariot "Of Turquoise blue and Em'rald Green," are intended to suggest the actual Welsh stream. In representing paradise Milton's problem was to show nature perfected without making it unbelievable. We are asked to take some things on faith: thornless roses, an unvarying climate, fruit of "golden rind." Yet these features are part of an idealized scene that can stand for a heightened version of the nature we know.

It should be recognized that while this walled, mountaintop garden is traditional, Milton reshaped the tradition of the earthly paradise. No one would confuse Milton's earthly paradise with Dante's, a *locus amoenus* in the medieval manner, with all the elements of the ideal landscape: trees and fragrant flowers, fresh water, birds singing, a gentle breeze.[4] Dante's paradise is charming because it is so delightfully naturalistic; it could be a typical spring scene if there were not clearly something marvelous in the atmosphere of the place and in the encounter of Dante and Matilda. Milton's garden offers not a "pleasance," as Dante's does, but a landscape more like the environs of Spenser's Bower of Bliss, as viewed by Guyon, with groves, streams, hills, and valleys.[5] Like

4. *Purgatorio,* 28.

5. *The Faerie Queene,* 1.12. Ernst Curtius defined the *topos* of the *locus amoenus* and enumerated the common characteristics of the ideal landscape (in *European Literature and the Latin Middle Ages,* trans. Willard Trask [New York, 1953], chap. 10). Curtius does not distinguish between varieties of the *locus amoenus* in terms of their spaciousness. One of the most important panoramic, or broad, landscapes is Virgil's Elysium (*Aeneid,* 6, 637ff.), in which the "locos laetos" in-

Spenser's false paradise, Eden is shown through the eyes of an antagonistic visitor who is nevertheless susceptible to the allure of the place; its depiction includes conventional earthly paradise motifs as well as all the pleasures of nature that the author can represent. For Spenser, of course, these natural delights are flawed by the artifice behind them. In many ways Milton's Eden is closer to Spenser's true paradise, the Garden of Adonis, where both harvest and spring are "continuall," decking with fresh colors the "wanton pryme," and where "all plenty and all pleasure flowes."[6]

Yet Milton's handling of the familiar materials is distinctly original. For example, he seldom resorts to the rhetorical device that Patch has called the "negative formula," by which such discomforts as disease and old

---

clude meadows, vales, groves, and fresh streams. The view that Musaeus shows Aeneas from a ridge of gleaming fields or plains ("camposque nitentis") extending below gives a sense of the amplitude of the place. The descriptions of heaven and paradise, summarized by Howard Rollins Patch in *The Other World* (Cambridge, Mass., 1950), frequently involve a meadow or plain, often a plateau at the top of a mountain. Spenser associated delight with broad landscapes in *The Faerie Queene* on several important occasions, perhaps thinking of Virgil as well as traditional representations of paradise or false paradises. On the top of Mount Acidale is "a spacious plaine" (6.100.8). Guyon and the Palmer, once past the gate, emerge into "a larger space / That stretcht it selfe into an ample plaine" (2.7.20–21). Tasso's Armida is to be found on a "pian su l'monte ampio ed aperto" (*Gerusalemme Liberata,* 15.53). Milton pictured his Garden as a "plain" at the top of a "woody Mountain" (8.303) and emphasized its extent, but spaciousness is linked with delight most notably in the description of heaven, with its vast plains.

6. *F.Q.,* 3.6. Quotations of Spenser's poetry are from *The Poetical Works of Edmund Spenser,* ed. J. C. Smith and E. De Selincourt (London, 1940).

age are specifically excluded from the earthly paradise.[7] This technique, which can be found in Homer's account of Olympus in the *Odyssey*—and countless subsequent descriptions of Elysium, the Golden Age, the Fortunate Isles, and the earthly paradise—can be illustrated by the earthly paradise of the fifth-century African, Dracontius:

> *In sun's hot rays it burneth not, by blasts*
> *Is never shaken, nor doth whirlwind rage*
> *With fierce-conspiring gales; no ice can quell,*
> *No hailstorm strike, nor under hoary frost*
> *Grow white the fields.*[8]

Instead of defining his Eden by exclusions, Milton overwhelms us with its sensuous appeal, avoiding details from the fallen world that would cloud our perception of the place itself. We do not hear of "pinching cold and scorching heate" (10. 691), storms, or Boreas and Thrascias and the rest of the company of the winds, until after the Fall, when they have become a reality. This minor deviation from tradition is characteristic of Milton's effort to avoid unnecessary rhetorical trappings in his description of Eden. However conventional his subject, he could at least present old motifs in new ways, working them into a freshly conceived vision of the place.

Milton's paradise is never static, or simply pictorial, as so many others are, because everything in his description works to lead the reader into the "Garden of bliss" and make him participate in delight. He conveys this delight partly through the conversations of Adam and Eve

7. *The Other World,* pp. 12–13.

8. *De Laudibus Dei,* 1, 190–94, as translated by Eleanor S. Duckett, *Latin Writers of the Fifth Century* (New York, 1930), p. 85.

and the series of tableaux in which he shows them, partly by presenting the features of the Garden in convincing ways rather than declaring their existence in the manner of someone proving the authenticity of his version of the myth by trotting out the familiar properties. We know that the trees of the Garden bear golden fruit and are perpetually in flower because we see them as they actually appear to Satan ("Blossoms and Fruits at once of golden hue / Appeerd" [4. 148]). The detail derived from patristic tradition, "and without Thorn the Rose" (4. 256), merely adds the final touch to a line that subtly lifts the description into the realm of the miraculous:

> *or the flourie lap*
> *Of som irriguous Valley spred her store,*
> Flours of all hue, and without Thorn the Rose.
> (4. 254–57)

Most references to eternal spring in accounts of the earthly paradise or the Golden Age are only slightly more elaborate than the Ovidian assertion, "Ver erat aeternum."[9] But Milton makes "Universal *Pan* / Knit with the *Graces* and the *Hours*" (4. 266–67) lead "Eternal Spring" in a graceful dance that complements the harmony of trembling leaves and the songs of the birds: an expression of the vibrant life of the Garden as well as an emblem of order. Nature is perpetually fresh and growing in Eden, as if always in the first hour of existence; each morning the plants "spring" with new life from the un-

9. *Metamorphoses,* 1.107. Compare Avitus' "Hic ver assiduum coeli clementia servat," J. P. Migne, *Patrologia Latina,* 59, 327, and Grotius' "Verque perpetuum gravem / Defendit hyemem," in *Adamus Exsul,* trans. Kirkconnell, *The Celestial Cycle,* p. 100.

believably fertile soil. Even the flowers seem alive, not static or decorative. In most ideal landscapes flowers are said to enamel, or paint, meadows and fields; comparisons with tapestry are frequent. But Milton makes his flowers a manifestation of the abundance of paradise and thus another proof of God's bounty:

> *Flours worthy of Paradise which not nice Art*
> *In Beds and curious Knots, but Nature boon*
> *Pour'd forth profuse on Hill and Dale and Plain.*
> (4. 241–43)

At one point Adam and Eve are shown reclining on a "soft downie Bank *damaskt* with flours" (4. 334), but the description of Adam sitting "On a green shadie Bank *profuse* of Flours" (8. 286) is more characteristic of Milton's manner in *Paradise Lost.*

The fragrance of the Garden more than any other traditional feature communicates a sense of intense and inescapable sensuous delight. Milton goes far beyond the customary brief reference to rich odors. Fragrance, from the omnipresent flowers and the heavier, more exotic scent of "Groves whose rich Trees wept odorous Gumms and Balme" (4. 248), is for him synonymous with delight. When Raphael enters the "spicie Forrest" on his way to Adam, it is as if he has entered a region, or state, of bliss:

> *Thir glittring Tents he passd, and now is come*
> *Into the blissful field, through Groves of Myrrhe,*
> *And flouring Odours, Cassia, Nard, and Balme;*
> *A Wilderness of sweets; for Nature here*
> *Wantond as in her prime, and plaid at will*
> *Her Virgin Fancies, pouring forth more sweet,*
> *Wilde above rule or Art; enormous bliss.*
> (5. 291–97)

This is an active nature, gratifying the sense of smell with an irresistible profusion of odors. The air itself, "pure now purer" to Satan as he approaches the Garden, "to the heart inspires / Vernal delight and joy" (4. 154–55). Delight, like nature, is always vernal in the Garden; although Adam and Eve surely know some variation in their pleasures, Milton gives the impression that pleasure in some form is continuously in the process of being realized. Thomas Greene has argued that the spices of the Garden contribute to a "lulling heaviness" in its atmosphere and offer an "invitation to indolence,"[10] but this should be true only for someone not acclimatized to such a special atmosphere, like Satan or the fallen reader with his dulled senses. We have trouble accepting a higher order of sensuous pleasure than we know from experience, just as we may find it hard to be comfortable with a nature that is not domesticated but wantons "as in her prime." Excess can be alarming when we are taught to prefer moderation. Spenser's Bower of Bliss is suspect because art "too lavishly" adorns the meadow with flowers, but nature in Eden cannot be too lavish. Its energies should be wondered at, not questioned.

The dynamic character of Milton's Eden is apparent in the landscape as a whole. The scene presented in two long descriptive passages early in Book 4 is more convincing, for several reasons, than the panorama Spenser offers in the Bower of Bliss episode. The most obvious of these reasons is the sustained movement of Milton's blank verse. In one skillfully modulated sentence that extends for forty lines (4. 223–63) he directs the reader's vision over the landscape, moving from simple,

10. Cf. *The Descent from Heaven* (New Haven, 1963), p. 401.

geographical fact ("Southward through *Eden* went a River large") to the marvelous (brooks "Rolling on Orient Pearl and Sands of Gold," fruit with "Golden Rind") without violating the illusion of reality. The scene has spatial depth, as Spenser's does not, largely because it is presented as a prospect.[11] Milton brings Satan, and thus the reader, into the scene by stationing him on the Tree of Life, whereas Spenser simply sets Guyon aside before embarking on his *descriptio*. Moreover, Milton indicates the relationship of features to one another by continually shifting his perspective, providing what Sergei Eisenstein, in commenting on other passages from *Paradise Lost,* has called "cinematographic instructions."[12] Milton directs our attention to the course of the streams of the Garden and moves from sunny field to shady bower, from groves of spice trees to others of fruit trees. Interspersed are lawns and downs with grazing flocks, "palmie" hillocks, and valleys spreading their store of flowers. Elsewhere ("Another side") are "umbrageous Grots and Caves." By contrast, Spenser's landscapes seem two-dimensional, simple lists of features with little indications of spatial relationships:

11. Milton is more famous for his prospects that violate human scale in presenting immense vistas, as in Adam's view of "all Earth's kingdoms in thir Glory" (11.384) from the highest hill of paradise or the prospect of cities and empires that Satan shows Christ in *Paradise Regained.* The vogue of the prospect in the seventeenth century is discussed by B. Sprague Allen, *Tides in English Taste* (Cambridge, Mass., 1937), and more fully by Siegfried Korninger in *Die Naturauffassung in der Englischen Dichtung des 17. Jahrhunderts* (Vienna, 1956), chap. 9.

12. See *The Film Sense,* trans. Jay Leyda (New York, 1942), pp. 58–62.

*There the most daintie paradise on ground*
*It selfe doth offer to his sober eye,*
*In which all pleasures plenteously abownd,*
*And none does others happinesse enuye:*
*The painted flowres, the trees upshooting hye,*
*The dales for shade, the hilles for breathing space,*
*The trembling groues, the Christall running by;*
*And that which all faire works doth most aggrace,*
*The art, which all that wrought, appeared in no place.*[13]

Ariosto and Tasso are no better at suggesting space in a landscape scene, nor is Sidney, for all the subtle harmony of his descriptions:

> There were hilles which garnished their proud heights with stately trees: humble valleis, whose base estate semed comforted with refreshing of silver rivers: medows, enameld with al sorts of ey-pleasing floures: thickets, which being lined with most pleasant shade, were witnessed so to by the chereful deposition of many wel-tuned birds: each pasture stored with sheep feeding with sober security, while

13. *F.Q.*, 2.12.58. Compare the landscape before the Temple of Venus:

*Fresh shadowes, fit to shroud from sunny ray;*
*Faire lawnds, to take the sunne in season dew;*
*Sweet springs, in which a thousand Nymphs did play;*
*Soft rombling brookes, that gentle slomber drew;*
*High reared mounts, the lands about to vew;*
*Low looking dales, disloigned from common gaze;*
*Delightful bowres, to solace lovers trew;*
*False Labyrinthes, fond runners eyes to daze;*
*All which by nature made did nature selfe amaze.*
(*F.Q.*, 4.10.24)

> the pretty lambs with bleting oratory craved the dams comfort: here a shepheards boy piping, as though he should never be old: there a young shepherdesse knitting, and withal singing, and it seemed that her voice comforted her hands to work, and her hands kept time to her voices musick.[14]

To find a firmly outlined scene one must look to the seventeenth century, to Denham's stylized but reasonably accurate description of the topography of the Thames valley in "Cooper's Hill" (1642), which Dr. Johnson credited with establishing the genre of local poetry.[15]

Milton adapted the technique of presenting a "prospect" to the description of an imaginary scene, an ideal landscape as opposed to an idealized one drawn from an actual model. While he placed the Garden geographically, and marked its center and circumference, his landscape has a fluidity that Denham's and Pope's comparable one in "Windsor Forest" do not. Milton suggests the actuality of the Garden without allowing its contours to harden. Groves and bowers are not located precisely, nor are "Hill and Dale and Plaine." And the use of "or" as a

14. *The Countesse of Pembrokes Arcadia,* ed. Albert Feuillerat (Cambridge, 1963), I, 13.

15. Robert Arnold Aubin, in *Topographical Poetry in XVIII-Century England* (New York, 1936), discusses the contributions of Denham and his immediate predecessors. In Cooper's Hill and the lesser-known poems that anticipated it there is an attention to the outlines of particular scenes not to be found in Drayton's *Poly-Olbion,* where the topography of England is lovingly traced but never visualized. In the representation of ideal landscapes, Drayton's eclogues, William Browne's *Brittania's Pastorals,* and the works of Giles and Phineas Fletcher are not significantly different from Spenser.

connective makes the parts of the landscape seem interchangeable, as if to suggest that all views are equally pleasant:

*Betwixt them Lawns, or level Downs, and Flocks*
*Grazing the tender herb, were interpos'd,*
*Or palmie hillock, or the flourie lap*
*Of som irriguous Valley spred her store.*

(4. 252–55)

Once we are within the Garden the limiting wall disappears. Here are "*All* Trees of noblest kind for sight, smell, taste," "Flours of *all* hue"; as we are told at the very beginning of the description, Satan is "To *all* delight of human sense expos'd." Spenser insists that "all" pleasures abound in the Bower of Bliss, but Milton is more emphatic. He would have us imagine "more" than "Natures whole wealth," because the delights of the "blissful Paradise / Of God" are beyond measure. This landscape must have a sense of openness, of "Variety without end," that the topography of the Thames valley, or any identifiable place in the familiar world, cannot have.

Eden is also an ordered world in which, as Northrop Frye has suggested, we cannot lose our way.[16] Adam and Eve may wander anywhere in the landscape of the Garden without becoming disoriented; in this environment they would have continued "secure," both safe and without cares, if it had not been for the intrusion of Satan and for Eve's desire for knowledge beyond that gained from her life in the Garden. The order of the landscape is a

16. *The Return of Eden* (Toronto, 1965), p. 31.

matter of proportion and balance.[17] Upon first awaking, Adam discovers around him a scene of "Hill, Dale, shadie Woods, and sunnie Plaines" (8. 262). Even Satan sees in the landscape of the earth a "sweet interchange / Of Hill and Vallie, Rivers, Woods and Plaines" (9. 115–16). Because Milton provided a justification for this landscape in heaven ("for Earth hath this variety from Heav'n / Of pleasure situate in Hill and Dale" [6. 640–41]), topography becomes a manifestation of the order of the universe as well as a source of pleasure. It is the visible design of God.[18] Both Spenser and Sidney pair complementary landscape features, "High reared mounts" and "Low looking dales," but without emphasizing contrast as an ordering principle. Instead Spenser offers simple variety:

> *So all agreed through sweete diversity,*
> *This gardin to adorne with all variety.*[19]

A line from Joseph Beaumont's insistently allegorical description of Eden could be taken as a commentary on Milton's landscape:

> *Sweet* Order *with* Variety *did play.*[20]

17. Arnold Stein has written suggestively on the order of the Garden, which he describes as "great variety fulfilling itself in greater harmony." See *Answerable Style* (Minneapolis, 1953), pp. 64–66.

18. H. V. S. Ogden, in "The Principles of Variety and Contrast in Seventeenth Century Aesthetics, and Milton's Poetry," *Journal of the History of Ideas* 10 (1949):159–82, has demonstrated with great thoroughness that an emphasis upon multiplicity of detail in landscape painting and poetry gave way in the seventeenth century to a preference for variety ordered by contrast. He cites most of the passages quoted above, among others, to illustrate Milton's use of variety and contrast.

19. *F.Q.*, 2.12.59.

20. *Psyche* 6, 166. In *Complete Poems*, ed. A. B. Grosart, 2 vols. (Edinburgh, 1880).

The evolution of this sense of an ordered nature can be seen in Pope's careful balance of opposites in "Windsor Forest":

*Here Hills and Vales, the Woodland and the Plain,*
*Here Earth and Water seem to strive again,*
*Not Chaos-like together crush'd and bruis'd,*
*But as the World, harmoniously confus'd:*
*Where Order in Variety we see,*
*And where, tho' all things differ, all agree.*[21]

Milton has vegetation contribute to the order of his natural world in subtle ways. In the final movement of the magnificent account of creation the trees bring to perfection the landscape planned by God:

*With high woods the hills were crownd,*
*With tufts the vallies and each fountain side,*
*With borders long the Rivers.*
(8. 326–28)

Within the Garden trees are not scattered at random but form groves, alleys, and bowers (with shrubs and flowers). Such features could be found in contemporary gardens; Bacon, for one, included alleys and arbors in his prescription for an ideal garden.[22] To make gardeners of Adam and Eve, who labor to keep their paths and bowers "from Wilderness" (9. 244–45), Milton had to introduce human standards of orderliness. But in clearing their paths Adam

21. *Pastoral Poetry and An Essay on Criticism,* ed. E. Audra and Aubrey Williams (London and New Haven, 1961). Earl Wasserman sees in this passage "the ideal expression of physical Nature's one law of *concordia discors,* the active harmonizing of differences." See *The Subtler Language* (Baltimore, 1959), p. 103.
22. *Of Gardens* (1664).

and Eve do not control or shape nature, which remains "Wilde above rule or Art" (5. 297). Wherever Milton got the idea for his alleys of trees, he presents them as part of the order in the mind of God, one more example of the way in which God has combined order with delight in the Garden. How far one could go in the opposite direction can be seen from the excesses of Du Bartas, in whose Eden alleys and arbors are cluttered by "love-knots" of roses tended by angels and even a topiary maze ornamented with the shapes of satyrs, centaurs, whales, and "thousand other counterfaited corses."[23]

Milton's "sovran Planter" (4. 691) worked in less capricious ways. Helen Gardner has called Eden a "landscape garden" of the sort that reached perfection in the garden parks of the eighteenth century. I would prefer to think of Milton's paradise as a garden on a divine rather than a human scale, more extensive and wilder than even a garden conceived as "nature in miniature" could be.[24] It has affinities not only with previous representations of the earthly paradise but with the literary landscape of Arcadia, invented by Virgil[25] and rediscovered and elaborated by Boccaccio, Sannazzaro, and Bembo.[26] Milton's Eden shares with this idealized pastoral world common natural delights, flocks if not shepherds, and a harmony of human figures with their natural setting.

Arcadia, or its various equivalents in the pastoral

23. *The Complete Works of Joshua Sylvester,* ed. A. B. Grosart (London, 1880), 1:104.

24. *A Reading of "Paradise Lost"* (Oxford, 1965), p. 79.

25. See Bruno Snell's chapter, "Arcadia: The Discovery of a Spiritual Landscape," in *The Discovery of Mind,* trans. T. G. Rosenmeyer (Cambridge, Mass., 1953).

26. In Sannazzaro's *L'Arcadia* and Bembo's *Gli Asolani.*

poetry of the Renaissance, is among other things a place where life is easy; its inhabitants, like Adam and Eve, are often shown against a natural background in attitudes of repose. Adam and Eve, of course, enjoy their repose only after labor sufficient to make "ease / more easie" (4. 329–30). A scene such as the one in which Adam and Eve are shown reclining on a flowery bank ("Under a tuft of shade") eating their supper fruits is an example of what Ernst Curtius has called the "motif of bucolic repose."[27] He traces this motif to Virgil's first eclogue, which begins with Tityrus reclining under a beech tree playing his pipe, reflecting on the *otium* of the shepherd's life: "O Meliboee, deus nobis haec otia fecit." The farmers described in the *Georgics* possess a similar *otium*, a leisure that implies freedom from care:

> *at secura quies et nescia fallere vita,*
> *dives opum variarum, at latis otia fundis*
> *speluncae vivique lacus et frigida Tempe*
> *mugitusque boum mollesque sub arbore somni*
> *non absunt.*[28]

The comparable sense of *secura quies* in the pastoral poetry of the Renaissance derives from the way figures are related to their landscape. If one needs an emblem to represent the Arcadian world, it should be a reclining or

27. In *European Literature and the Latin Middle Ages*, p. 191.

28. *Georgics*, 2, 467–71:

> Yet theirs is repose without care, and a life that knows no fraud, but is rich in treasures manifold. Yea, the ease of broad domains, caverns, and living lakes, and cool vales, the lowing of the kine, and soft slumbers beneath the trees—all are theirs. (Trans. H. R. Fairclough, *Loeb Classical Library*)

seated figure, suggesting by his relaxation and his harmony with nature a profound calmness of mind.[29] Milton's tableau is perhaps the richest statement of this motif in English poetry. Yet the frisking about of all the animals around Adam and Eve in itself sufficiently reveals that their "ease" goes beyond the *otium* of pastoral poetry. As Adam is reminded in his discourse with Raphael on astronomy, their contentment depends upon obedience. He is taught to live

*The easiest way, nor with perplexing thoughts*
*To interrupt the sweet of Life, from which*
*God hath bid dwell farr off all anxious cares,*
*And not molest us, unless we our selves*
*Seek them with wandring thoughts, and notions vaine.*
(8. 183–87)

There is little emphasis on the repose of Adam and Eve in the tradition of the earthly paradise before Milton; the closest thing to it is the enervating repose shown in the false paradises of Ariosto, Tasso, and Spenser. But there is one notable presentation of a pastoral Eden in hexaemeral drama, Giambattista Andreini's *L'Adamo* (1613). Andreini skillfully relates Adam and Eve to a lush natural setting and, like Milton, compares Eve with

29. Spenser and Drayton provide characteristic examples of the motif:

*The gentle shepheard satte beside a springe,*
*All in the shadowe of a bushye brere.*
"December," *The Shepheardes Calender*

*In delights that never fade,*
*The Muses lulled be,*
*And sit at pleasure in the shade*
*Of many a stately tree.*
"The Muses Elizium"

flowers and pictures her among them. His most sophisticated use of natural description is in the scene in which he shows Adam greeting Eve on her return, unaware that she had sinned. Adam enthusiastically points out to Eve an enticing stream that flows through a meadow and then falls to a "deep and fruitful vale, / With laurel crown'd and olive, / With cypresses, oranges, and lofty pines," inviting her to enjoy with him the newly discovered prospect:

> *Now by these cooling shades,*
> *The beauty of these plants,*
> *By these delightful meadows,*
> *These variegated flowers,*
> *By the soft music of the rills and birds*
> *Let us sit down in joy!*[30]

The closest visual analogues to Milton's Eden are probably the ideal landscapes of such painters as Giorgione, Titian,[31] Claude, and Poussin[32] portraying an

30. Trans. William Cowper, *Complete Poetical Works* (New York, 1848), 1:767.

31. A. Richard Turner, in *The Vision of Landscape in Renaissance Italy* (Princeton, 1966), 119ff., relates the pastoral landscapes of Giorgione and Titian to the contemporary literary vogue of Arcadia.

32. Poussin's landscapes are probably the most like Milton's. His *Spring* is unlike most representations of Eden in not being dominated by Adam and Eve and the serpent. Adam and Eve appear as relatively small figures set in a green world in which trees and often space alternate and several vistas open into the distance. Sir Kenneth Clark, in *Landscape into Art* (London, 1949), pp. 68–69, briefly compares Poussin with Milton and calls his *Spring* a "perfect illustration for *Paradise Lost*." Mario Praz's comparison of Milton and Poussin focuses on parallels in the artistic development of the two men. See "Milton and Poussin," in *Seventeenth Century Studies Presented to Sir Herbert Grierson* (Oxford, 1938), pp. 192–210.

Arcadian landscape. The comparison seems to me worth making, if only to suggest how pervasive the feeling for an Arcadian world was. In certain landscapes of all of these painters one seems to escape the actual countryside of the Roman campagna into a timeless, extraordinarily peaceful world where goddesses and nymphs do not seem out of place. In Giorgione's *Sleeping Venus,* for example, the nude goddess reclines under a tree in perfect harmony with the landscape that extends behind her.[33] Milton's natural world before the Fall is "a seat where Gods might dwell, / Or wander with delight" (7. 329–30)—not pagan gods, of course, but angels and archangels. In short, Eden appears as a Christianized Arcadia.

The tranquillity of the landscape scenes of the painters I have mentioned is sometimes on the verge of disruption, as in Giorgione's *The Tempest,* in which a thunderstorm is about to break in the background. Poussin has a number of paintings in which an Arcadian world is threatened: *Orpheus and Eurydice,* which shows Eurydice about to be bitten by a snake; *Apollo and Daphne,* with Cupid aiming an arrow at Apollo; *Landscape with a Snake,* in which a snake is shown with its victim in one corner of the scene. The two paintings on the theme *Et in Arcadia Ego* dramatically introduce the presence of death into a tranquil pastoral world.[34] The elegiac note in such paintings, and in *Paradise Lost,* where Eden is rarely seen without ominous shadows, belongs to a more sophisti-

33. See *The Vision of Landscape in Renaissance Italy,* pp. 94–95, for an excellent discussion of the "Arcadian mood" of this painting.

34. For Erwin Panofsky's explanation of the significance of the inscription, see *Et In Arcadia Ego:* Poussin and the Elegiac Tradition," *Meaning in the Visual Arts* (New York, 1955), pp. 295–320.

cated kind of pastoral than simple portrayals of rustic life. Under the threat of disruption or death the pastoral ideal can stand for more than an escape from the strain and moral ambiguities of city or court. It is not so much a pleasant fiction as a poignant image of what life might have been.

The elegiac mood that so strongly colors our response to Eden extends to other descriptive passages in *Paradise Lost.* The vision of blissful life on the stars that Satan passes in his journey to the earth is powerful precisely because it is illusory—for him and, by implication, for anyone. The outline of an ideal landscape embodies general human yearnings for a simple happiness:

> *Or other Worlds they seem'd, or happy Iles,*
> *Like those* Hesperian *Gardens fam'd of old,*
> *Fortunate Fields, and Groves and flourie Vales.*
> (8. 567–69)

The sense of loss is like an undertow in the first book of the poem, strongest in the description of Satan's despair but reasserting itself in the catalogue of pagan gods. Having lost the "happy Fields" of heaven, the fallen angels will corrupt the appealing places of the earth, such as the "pleasant Vally of *Hinnom*" (1. 404), desecrated by the worship of Baal and transformed into "black *Gehenna*," the "Type of Hell." Fair Damascus, "on the fertil Banks / Of *Abbana* and *Pharphar,* lucid streams" (1. 468–69), becomes Rimmon's "delightful Seat." Even the reference to the "flowry Dale of *Sibma* clad with Vines" (1. 410) is elegiac, since these vineyards were destroyed as a punishment for Moab's pride (Is. 16:8).

The most alluring landscape of the first two books appears in the pastoral simile with which Milton marks the agreement of the fallen angels, beautifully evoking the harmony of nature after a storm:

> *If chance the radiant Sun with farewell sweet*
> *Extend his ev'ning beam, the fields revive,*
> *The birds thir notes renew, and bleating herds*
> *Attest thir joy, that hill and valley rings.*
>
> (2. 492–95)

If the simile were merely an illustration of the concord of "Devil with Devil damn'd," its power would seem strangely out of proportion to the scene in hell, but much more is involved. This moment of tranquillity, comparable to scenes of harmony in Eden, stands for a peace apparently beyond the reach of men, who, "though under hope / Of heavenly Grace,"

> *Yet live in hatred, enmity, and strife*
> *Among themselves, and levie cruel warres,*
> *Wasting the Earth, each other to destroy.*
>
> (2. 500–502)

And yet one ideal landscape in *Paradise Lost* suggests an attainable ideal. This is Milton's affirmation of his poetic power in the invocation to Book 3:

> *Yet not the more*
> *Cease I to wander where the Muses haunt*
> *Cleer Spring, or shadie Grove, or Sunnie Hill,*
> *Smit with the love of sacred Song; but chief*
> *Thee* Sion *and the flowrie Brooks beneath*
> *That wash thy hallowd feet, and warbling flow,*
> *Nightly I visit.*
>
> (3. 26–32)

These scenes are more than a shorthand way of referring

to places of inspiration. They are landscapes of the imagination where Milton finds something of the clarity and assurance suggested by the landscapes of Eden, though not the innocence. In this ideal world the poet has his bearings and can wander without fear of losing his way.

The true image of perfection in *Paradise Lost* is heaven. Although the landscape of Eden is much more fully and convincingly realized, it can only be regarded as a "shadow" of the hills and valleys of heaven, which stand for a bliss beyond the threat of change. The landscapes of heaven vary according to Milton's purposes. The region within the walls appears in one perspective as a vast plain, in another as a configuration of hill and valley. Still closer to the throne of God is the "river of Bliss," Milton's adaptation of the river of life briefly pictured in Revelation.

> *[Immortal Amarant] there grows,*
> *And flours aloft shading the Fount of Life,*
> *And where the river of Bliss through midst of Heavn*
> *Rowls o'er Elisian Flours her Amber stream.*
> (3. 356–59)

Although it threatens to become purely allegorical, this river, with its surrounding flowers, more nearly suggests a natural scene than the river of Revelation or Dante's river of light.[35] Where Dante emphasized the discontinuity between heaven and paradise, Milton in this scene and in the one revealing the angels taking their supper while reclining on flowers made the resemblances between the two places obvious enough for heaven to seem the model for Eden in significant ways. Since heaven has

35. *Paradiso*, 30.

a visible and substantial landscape, however brief our glimpses of it, we can imagine the order and delight that Adam and Eve find in nature as a reflection of celestial harmony.

The celestial hills and valleys are more obviously symbolic than their earthly counterparts. The strongest image that Milton coud find for the "horrible confusion" (6. 668) introduced into heaven by war was the uprooting of these hills. The restoration of the landscape is proof of the Son's power to bring about a renewal of order:

> *Heav'n his wonted face renewd,*
> *And with fresh Flourets Hill and Valley smil'd.*
> (6. 783–84)

As in the pastoral simile of Book 2, the phrase "Hill and Valley" is a formula suggesting the return of harmony. Satan's references to heaven's "happy Fields" (1. 249) and the "Vales of Heav'n" (1. 321) reflect visions of lost bliss and ease. In Eve's regret at losing the "happie Walks and Shades" (9. 270) of the Garden and Adam's nostalgic account of the places where he saw God, the landscape mirrors feelings in a similar way, reinforcing the sense that the bliss of paradise anticipates that of heaven.

Yet we can more nearly measure the landscape and the joys of paradise than we can those of heaven. The immensity of heaven, as Milton pictures it, daunts the imagination. We know that heaven is traditionally square because Milton refers to it as God's "Quadrature" (10. 381), but Satan, who sees the wall in the distance "extended wide / In circuit, undetermined square or round" (2. 1048), cannot find its limits. The plain within the walls extends so far that Abdiel travels all night through "Heav'ns wide Champain" (6. 2) returning from Satan's newly established kingdom in the "spacious North" (5. 726); on the following day the faithful angels make the same journey in reverse, marching over "many a Province wide / Tenfold the length of this terrene" (6. 77). Even in the description of the angels at rest we are made aware of the vastness of heaven:

> *Wide over all the Plain, and wider farr*
> *Than all this globous Earth in Plain out spred,*
> *(Such are the Courts of God) Th'Angelic throng*
> *Disperst in Bands and Files thir Camp extend*
> *By living Streams among the Trees of Life,*
> *Pavilions numberless.*
>
> (5. 648–53)

These incalculable numbers and distances suggest unbounded freedom and joy and a security that does not depend upon particular walks and bowers. It is meaningless to talk of angels losing their way in heaven.

These horizontal measurements invite comparison with the predominantly vertical measurements of hell, which indicate pride and ambition. The wide extension of heaven suggests that although Milton's cosmos has a ceiling, its size can no more be appreciated by the human mind than can the power and knowledge of God. We are not conscious of the size of the faithful angels because they are diminished by their environment. It is the self-assertive fallen angels who stand out against their background, in postures of defiance.

In its landscape as in so many other ways hell parodies heaven. Milton frequently refers to hell in terms that suggest moral and psychological rather than physical dimensions. As a "deep world / Of darkness" (2. 262–63), it seems impossibly removed from divine favor; as a "dark opprobrious Den of shame" (2. 58), it is a place where the unseemliness of rebellion can be kept from view; as the "infernal Vaile" (2. 742), it suggests a perversion of the repose of heaven. The external scene seems no more than a projection of spiritual realities when Satan first looks around him and sees "Regions of sorrow, doleful shades, where peace / And rest can never dwell" (1. 65–66). Yet Milton does give hell a discernible landscape, or rather a series of landscapes.[36] What Satan first sees as "The dismal Situation waste and wilde" (1. 60), he later refers to as "Yon dreary Plain, forlorn and wilde" (1. 180). This desolate plain, insofar as it is visible through the gloom, suggests that there is no relief or escape from their condition for Satan and his legions. When vistas open up in hell, they only offer more reasons for despair. The fallen angels can never lose for long the oppressive sense of confinement that Satan describes:

> *Our prison strong, this huge convex of Fire,*
> *Outrageous to devour, immures us round*
> *Ninefold, and gates of burning Adamant*
> *Barr'd over us prohibit all egress.*
>
> (2. 434–37)

Many of the features of the infernal landscape serve a specific occasion. A volcano provides gold for the building of Pandaemonium. A plain is available for the fallen angels who engage in heroic games while Satan is away; there are "Rocks and Hills" (2. 540) on which others can

36. Marjorie Nicolson, *John Milton: A Reader's Guide to his Poetry* (New York, 1963), pp. 193–200, distinguishes three hells: the landscape that Satan sees upon arising from the burning lake, which she suggests is based upon the Phlegraean Fields near Naples; Pandemonium; and the world that the fallen angels explore in Satan's absence.

vent their rage; others can sing their own deeds in a "silent valley" (2. 547). Those who set out "On bold adventure to discover wide / That dismal world" (2. 571–72), proceeding away from the burning lake along the four rivers of hell, find no "easier habitation" but a "Universe of death" (2. 622). Contrasts between the barrenness of hell and Eden's fertility are reinforced by topographical differences. The exploring angels pass through "many a dark and dreary Vale" and over "many a Frozen, many a fierie Alpe," but these have no relation to each other and seem a grotesque distortion of the hills and dales of the earth. There is no apparent order to the "Rocks, Caves, Lakes, Fens, Bogs, Dens, and shades of death" (2. 261) that make up this inhospitable world.[37] In the "frozen Continent" found in another part of hell the familiar landscape features are entirely obliterated.

37. Marjorie Nicolson, *Mountain Gloom and Mountain Glory* (Ithaca, N.Y., 1959), chap. 1, has shown that seventeenth-century English poets took their mountains from literary tradition, describing them as desolate and inhospitable in the manner of Roman poets.The mountainsof hell are completely forbidding, as are the "Alpine mountains cold" of Milton's sonnet on the Piedmontese massacre. They are also monstrous in their asymmetry. As Miss Nicolson points out (p. 69), using Marvell's "Upon Appleton House" by way of illustration, beauty was at this time "a mean between extremes, appealing to Reason that recognized proportion, limitation, and restraint as qualities imposed by God upon nature when he brought order out of chaos." In Milton's account of the creation the height of mountains is balanced by the depth of the seas: "So high as heav'd the tumid Hills, so low / Down sunk a hollow bottom broad and deep, / Capacious bed of Waters" (7. 288–90).

The wild landscape of hell, though initially shocking to the fallen angels, seems an appropriate setting for demonic forces. Its affinities are with the more sinister haunted landscapes of epic and romance: meres, caves, deserts.

*Beyond this flood a frozen Continent*
*Lies dark and wilde, beat with perpetual storms*
*Of Whirlwind and dire Hail, which on firm land*
*Thaws not, but gathers heap, and ruin seems*
*Of ancient pile; all else deep snow and ice,*
*A gulf profound as that* Serbonian *Bog*
*Betwixt* Damiata *and mount* Casius *old,*
*Where Armies whole have sunk.*

(2. 587–94)

In a poem about the loss of Eden the image of the "happie Garden" (3. 66) could not persist unchanged to the end, at least when landscape is never merely neutral background. The Garden itself does not change immediately, only Adam's perception of it in his new self-consciousness and guilt. In his imagination the place is not only disordered ("these wilde Woods forlorn" [9. 910]), but shrunk to the "glade / Obscur'd" (10. 1084–85) where he would like to live in solitude. In the broadest sense Eden ceases to exist from the moment in which it becomes for Adam a place in which to hide. The sudden transformation of the Garden in Adam's mind dramatically reveals how completely his original harmony with his surroundings depended upon harmony with God. As a consequence of his isolation from God, and from Eve, Eden loses its meaning.

Adam can renew his love for Eve and appeal to God for mercy, but the divorce between heaven and earth reflected in actual changes in the natural world is permanent. In his treatment of these changes, a standard theme of hexaemeral literature, Milton placed particular emphasis on the ravaging of the Garden. The most disturbing image of change is that of Death ready to devour herb, fruit, flower, and "whatever thing / The Scythe of Time mows down" (10. 605–606). This is Milton's version of the tombstone in Arcadia, only his Eden, unlike the fictionalized world of shepherds and flocks, cannot absorb the presence of death. His pastoral world is devastated not only by time but by the winds, by the heat of the flaming sword, and ultimately by the flood. Adam actually sees the winds (which include "*Zephir*," the normally gentle west wind always present in the earthly paradise) "shattering the graceful locks / Of these fair spreading Trees" (10. 1066–67). Michael's preview of the final destruction of paradise demonstrates to Adam as nothing else could that the bliss of Eden is irrevocably lost.

> *then shall this Mount*
> *Of Paradise by might of Waves be moovd*
> *Out of his place, pushd by the horned floud,*
> *With all his verdure spoil'd, and Trees adrift*
> *Down the great River to th'op'ning Gulf,*
> *And there take root an Iland salt and bare,*
> *The haunt of Seales and Orcs, and Sea-mews clang.*
> (11. 829–35)

The lesson of the scene, as Michael expounds it, is that "God attributes to place / No sanctitie" (11. 836–37). This is an essential part of Adam's education—if he is to create a new order for himself, he must not look back nostalgically to Eden—yet the vision is almost unendurable. The trees that formed stately alleys are set "adrift," as the hill of paradise is dislodged and swept away. Milton used a similar image and virtually the same rhythm in another powerful evocation of disorder, his description in *Lycidas* of the head of the murdered Orpheus being carried "Down the swift *Hebrus* to the *Lesbian* shore." The destruction is all the more frightening in *Paradise Lost* because it is unleashed by God. Paradise itself, by a kind of brutal realism that denies the validity of myth, is transformed from an ideal world into an actual place, an "Iland salt and bare" of the sort reported by travellers.[38]

Adam's first view of the world in which he finds himself before being taken up to Eden is a delightful scene of "Hill, Dale, and shady Woods, and sunny Plains / And liquid Lapse of murmuring Streams" (8. 262–63). While there is no reason to believe that this topography changes after the Fall, Milton could not very well picture again the interchange of hill and valley, with its connotations of pleasure and security. Instead he developed a contrast between the mount of paradise (and implicitly the delight, ease, and familiarity with God for which it stands) and a "lower World" (11. 283), a "subjected Plaine" (12. 640) where a man dominates his surroundings instead of blending into them. Scenes of lust, ambition, and violence blot out the natural world, which Milton typically shows as a plain.

> *So violence*
> *Proceeded, and Oppression, and Sword-Law*
> *Through all the Plain, and refuge none was found.*
> (11. 671–73)

This plain, into which Adam and Eve venture at the end of the poem, is sometimes the setting for pastoral scenes, but these are invariably disrupted: by Cain, by Nim-

38. See Broadbent, *Some Graver Subject* (New York, 1960), p. 273 n., for examples.

rod, or by giants who attack the shepherds and scatter their flocks. Michael assures Adam that although he is "brought down / To dwell on even ground" with his sons (12. 347–48) God's presence will be found "In Vallie and in plaine" (11. 349). Yet the overwhelming impression of the last two books is that man cannot look for any real refuge in the wilderness of this world; Milton's austere view of life after the Fall permits no more "happy Walks and Shades" (11. 270).

The point of Michael's harsh lessons in history is not to intensify the memory of life in paradise but to wrench Adam's thoughts away from Eden. Michael's purpose is to bring Adam to accept the "lower world" and to recognize that henceforth struggle and not rest will be the basic condition of life in it. Adam must learn not to look to his natural surroundings for confirmation of God's benevolence and his own well-being as he did in the Garden. In his new understanding Eden is a type of the heavenly paradise that awaits the faithful. Meanwhile, he can find consolation, if he has faith and the strength to act upon it, in the "paradise within" that each individual can win for himself. Milton no doubt would agree with Richard Sibbes's assertion that "faith makes quiet the soul."[39] An inner peace, stronger than the peace of Eden because self-attained and independent of the external world, is the faithful man's reward in this life.

39. See Richard Sibbes, *Light from Heaven* (London, 1638), p. 138. In his *Christian Doctrine,* CE, 16:49, Milton relates the "peace of God, which passeth all understanding" (Phil. 4:7) to the individual's sense of justification: "From a consciousness of justification proceed peace and real tranquility of mind."

# 3
# HEAVEN

Milton's heaven has never interested commentators on *Paradise Lost* the way hell and Eden have. The dialogue of Father and Son in Book 3 and the grand battles of Books 5 and 6 have received their share of attention, but the setting for these episodes, the place itself, is generally ignored, or dismissed with a few words of apology or censure. Reasons are not hard to find. We see heaven fitfully, in scattered glimpses of battlements, flowers, and angel choruses, not steadily and whole as we see the Garden. In representing heaven, furthermore Milton was bound by the evidence of Revelation. As Helen Gardner has observed, one reason that Milton "wrote in fetters" when he wrote of heaven is that he could regard the biblical description of the elaborate New Jerusalem only as inspired by God.[1] The varied literary tradition of the earthly paradise, however, in which details from Genesis play a relatively small part, allowed Milton much greater freedom to develop Eden to suit his dramatic purposes.

Yet Milton's heaven is not as fragmented or unoriginal

1. *A Reading of "Paradise Lost"* (Oxford, 1965), p. 55.

as it may at first seem. The details taken over from Revelation—jewelled walls and towers, the river of life, and the rest—are carefully worked into the fabric of the poem. And the heaven of *Paradise Lost* has one important aspect that owes relatively little to Revelation. It is among other things a pastoral heaven, where the angels enjoy their meals "On flours reposed" (5. 634) and take their leisure in "blissful Bowrs" (11. 77). Milton followed the lead of Revelation in fusing the city of God and the celestial paradise but varied the proportions to give the paradisal aspect of heaven much greater significance than it assumes in the Bible. This emphasis is not surprising in view of the pattern of correspondences in *Paradise Lost.*

Milton achieved one of the fullest literary representations of heaven outside *The Divine Comedy* and certainly the finest. The immense difficulties of describing the unknowable were enough to restrain most attempts and to prompt numerous confessions of insufficiency.[2] Dante several times in the *Paradiso* claims that the task is too great for his art, and Milton acknowledges through Raphael the difficulty of showing "what surmounts the reach / Of human sense" (5. 571–72). Both poets nevertheless risked picturing heaven: Dante through a schematic design and bold images, Milton through a series of scenes and hints of scenes. Descriptions of heaven in Renaissance epics before *Paradise Lost* are slight and often more classical than Christian in manner.

The admiration of Sannazzaro and Vida for the clas-

2. See C. A. Patrides, *Milton and the Christian Tradition* (Oxford, 1966), pp. 282–83, for a brief discussion of the attitudes of Christian apologists toward the problem of picturing heaven. Patrides notes that one method was "to resort to the *theologia negativa,* to state what will *not* be found in Heaven."

sical epic, particularly the *Aeneid,* was too strong for them to pay much attention to the model provided by Revelation, even though their subjects were explicitly Christian. In Sannazzaro's *De Partu Virginis* and Vida's *Christiad* heaven is referred to as Olympus.[3] In Sannazzaro's epic the blessed wonder at the golden walls of the holy city and its golden houses with jewelled roofs.[4] As Thomas Greene has pointed out, his God appears as "a kind of Renaissance prince with angels for courtiers, each angel assigned to his own palace, each palazzo bearing its owner's name and heraldic arms."[5] Vida's heaven is also a realm of light where the angels live in golden palaces. In the only sustained descriptive passage that does not have to do with the war in heaven, he presents an image of royal state that Milton might have thought more appropriate to Satan:

> *There stands a temple, glorious to behold,*
> *Built of eternal adamant and gold,*
> *High o'er the vault of stars in heav'ns abode,*
> *The sumptuous palace of the sov'reign God:*
> *I'th'midst a mount; whose top aspiring high,*
> *Cleaves, like a tap'ring pyramid, the sky:*
> *Unnumber'd seats, in various ranks dispos'd,*
> *Above, beneath, the sacred mount inclos'd.*
> *Hither advanc'd awhile th'angelic throng,*
> *And prais'd their Monarch in the dance and song;*

3. Milton referred to heaven as Olympus in his early poems and imagined himself looking in on a Homeric heaven in *At a Vacation Exercise.*

4. *De Partu Virginis,* ed. Antonio Altamura (Naples, 1948), I, 444–52.

5. *The Descent from Heaven* (New Haven, Conn., 1963), p. 157.

*They all, attentive to precedence, sate*
*In thrice three circles round the throne of state.*[6]

Milton, who avoided making his heaven too concrete, neither seats his angels nor numbers the ranks of the celestial assembly:

*In Orbes*
*Of circuit inexpressible they stood,*
*Orb within Orb.*

(5. 594–96)

The conclave in hell, with "A thousand Demy-Gods on golden seat's" (1. 796), is more like political gatherings we know.

Milton could have found a much fuller and more decisively Christian heaven in Tasso's revised version of the *Gerusalemme Liberata,* the *Gerusalemme Conquistata,* and in his hexaemeron, *Il Mondo Creato.* In the latter Tasso stresses the "riposo eterno" of the blessed, a repose joined with "gloria" and "pompa trionfal."[7] Tasso's emphasis on the splendor of heaven and the pomp of the divine court is more pronounced in the vision of heaven that he added to his epic in the process of infusing it with the spirit of the Counter Reformation.[8] The heaven that Goffredo beholds, like that of *Il Mondo Creato,* is free from tempest and war and enjoys eternal spring. There is a river of light (one is frequently reminded of Dante) bordered by a wood that offers fruit and shade. Yet the dazzling radiance that Tasso gives to

6. *The Christiad,* trans. J. Cranwell (Cambridge, Eng., 1768), p. 301.

7. *Il Mondo Creato,* ed. Georgio Petrocchi (Florence, 1951), 7, 397–400, 423.

8. *Gerusalemme Conquistata,* 20.

city, golden stars, angels, and God overwhelms this suggestion of a landscape. The city itself is crowned with high towers and a "superbi fronti" and adorned, like a "sposa real," with rare gems and gold. Tasso devotes several stanzas to enumerating the various jewels and capturing the effect of their shimmering reflections. By comparison Milton's descriptions of celestial splendor seem muted.

Spenser pictured a Christian heaven in the conclusion to the November eclogue of *The Shepheardes Calender,* in scattered stanzas of *An Hymne of Heavenly Love,* and in a few lines devoted to the New Jerusalem in Book 1 of *The Faerie Queene* (10.55). But his admirer Giles Fletcher offered a much fuller vision of heaven in *Christ's Victorie and Triumph.* Fletcher places the "holy Cittie" in a setting that resembles the earthly paradise, with eternal spring, flowers and fruit together on the trees, and rivers of milk, wine, and honey. In his description of the angels (who pitch "round about in order glorious / Their sunny Tents, and houses luminous"),[9] Fletcher reminds one of Milton, though Milton's presentation of heaven is more unified and more dramatic. Another vision of heaven worth noticing is that of Joseph Beaumont's *Psyche.* Beaumont presents two versions of heaven, the first a "court of chastity," which includes a garden and a crystal castle presided over by Mary instead of Venus and by her son the "king of royal Chastity."[10] The second is dominated by the New Jerusalem, which Beaumont describes

9. Giles and Phineas Fletcher, *Poetical Works,* ed. F. S. Boas (Cambridge, Eng., 1908), 1:82.

10. *Complete Poems of Dr. Joseph Beaumont,* ed. A. B. Grosart (Edinburgh, 1880), 1:42–44.

with a dogged fidelity to Revelation, reproducing all the unwieldy details that Milton rejected.[11]

The biblical golden streets and jewelled walls are not to everyone's taste. John Donne, troubled by the conception of heaven as offering an improvement on the material benefits of this world, preferred to conceive of it abstractly as the place "wherein dwelleth Righteousness" (2 Pet. 3:13).[12] But Milton embraced the physical model, at least in its outlines, to make it embody the glory of God.[13] In *Paradise Lost,* as in the Bible, heavenly splendor dramatically excels anything to be found on earth. The biblical New Jerusalem as an idealized version of the actual Jerusalem[14] is specifically contrasted with Babylon, symbol of terrestrial riches and the moral corruption that they signify. The merchants' lament for their destroyed city is a lament for their lost wealth:

> Alas, alas, that great city, that was clothed in fine linen, and purple, and scarlet, and decked with gold, and precious stones, and pearls.
> (Rev. 18:6)

Milton returns again and again in *Paradise Lost* to the false magnificence of earthly riches: in the "*Barbaric* Pearl and Gold" (2. 4) that the "gorgeous East" showers on her kings; in the "gay Religions full of Pomp and

11. *Complete Poems,* 2:223–26.

12. "Funeral Sermon for Magdalen Danvers," *Sermons,* ed. Evelyn Simpson (Berkeley, Calif., 1953–62), 8:82.

13. Omitting all but one of the traditional twelve gates and greatly reducing the kinds of jewels.

14. See Austin Farrar, *The Revelation of St. John the Divine* (Oxford, 1964), pp. 214–23, on the correspondence between the earthly and the heavenly Jerusalems.

Gold" (I. 372); in the "Gems and wanton dress" (II. 583) of the daughters of Cain; but preeminently in Pandaemonium itself:

> *Not* Babilon,
> *Nor great* Alcairo *such magnificence*
> *Equal'd in all thir glories, to inshrine*
> Belus *or* Serapis *thir Gods, or seat*
> *Thir Kings, when* Aegypt *with* Assyria *strove*
> *In wealth and luxurie.*
>
> (I. 717–22)

Displays of wealth inevitably suggest avarice and vaingloriousness in *Paradise Lost*. In Satan's case they are also a sign of blasphemous presumption. Pandaemonium is a blatant attempt to rival the glory of heaven and Satan's palace in the north of heaven, stands as a symbol of monstrous pride,

> *far blazing, as a Mount*
> *Rais'd on a Mount, with Pyramids and Towrs*
> *From Diamond Quarries hew'n, and Rocks of Gold.*
>
> (5. 757–59)

It is impossible to conceive of either place without thinking of Satan's ambition.

In using the riches of heaven as a foil to the ostentatious luxury of the earth and a means of blazoning forth true majesty Milton was following the example of Revelation. His heaven seems materialistic only if we insist upon measuring it by earthly standards. The example of Mammon, fascinated with the golden pavement that the other angels do not seem to notice, indicates that what one sees depends upon the beholder. Milton emphasizes the radiant appearance of heaven's walls and towers, which gleam with reflected light. The bright pavement shines like a "sea of Jasper" (3. 363); the gate that Satan sees above him is resplendent:

> *Far more rich appeerd*
> *The work as of a Kingly Palace Gate*
> *With Frontispice of Diamond and Gold*
> *Imbellisht, thick with sparkling orient Gemmes*
> *The Portal shon.*
>
> (3. 504–508)

We can imagine the vast wall that confronts Satan as he emerges from Chaos, "With Opal Towrs and Battlements adorn'd / Of living Saphire" (2. 1049–50), dazzling the eye with its brightness. The brilliance of heaven has nothing to do with human estimates of value; these are simply the finest, and purest, materials conceivable.

Milton's conception of God as a king who enjoys royal state helps to explain his emphasis on the splendor of heaven. Some critics have felt that divine and earthly kingship are not sufficiently discriminated in *Paradise Lost* and that God is compromised by trappings of state.[15] But the same objections would have to be made to the Old Testament conception of God as supreme king and Lord of hosts and to the New Testament concern with the kingship of Christ. By making God the "Eternal King Omnipotent" Milton only echoed the Lord of the prophetic books, always ready to scatter the wicked. The contrast between God's omnipotence and the illusory power of Satan, the "Sultan" or "emperor" who antici-

15. Malcolm Ross has argued that Milton's heaven is not adequately distinguished from earthly monarchies; he prefers the simple majesty of Adam. See *Milton's Royalism* (Ithaca, N.Y., 1943), pp. 100–112. J. B. Broadbent has expressed his unhappiness with the idea of God as king and Milton's use of it. See *Some Graver Subject* (New York, 1960), pp. 225–28.

pates all earthly kings in his pomp and ambition, parallels the biblical contrast between the true King whose kingdom shall be without end and the succession of corrupt kings chronicled in the Old Testament. Such phrases as "Imperial Summons" (5. 583) and "Regal Power" (5. 739) when applied to heaven make it all the more clear that divine omnipotence transcends any ordinary military and political powers:

> *Who can impair thee, mighty King, or bound*
> *Thy Empire?*
>
> (7. 608–609)

So sing the angels celebrating the creation as they recall the defeat of Satan. Arthur Dent, writing in 1603, applauded a similar contrast between worldly and divine regality in the fourth chapter of Revelation, in which God appears enthroned:

> "Behold a throne, etc." Here beginneth the description of the most high and glorious majesty of God, who is described after the manner of earthly kings and judges sitting upon their thrones and judgment-seats. For he is King of Zion, and Judge of all the world.[16]

For Milton God's power is inseparable from his glory, and both are suggested by jewelled walls and glimpses of angelic forces arrayed for battle: "in Arms they stood / Of golden Panoplie, refulgent Host" (6. 526–27). In one aspect heaven is a fortress, whose impregnable battlements and inaccessible gate we see from the viewpoint of the banished Satan. But the paramount manifestation of divine power in *Paradise Lost* is the appearance of the

16. *The Ruin of Rome* (Glasgow, 1798; originally published in 1603), p. 80.

Son in the "Chariot of Paternal Deitie." The chariot with its brilliant jewels suggests an irresistible power that cannot be conceived of in ordinary human terms. Milton took the idea for this chariot from Ezekiel, but the episode owes something to Revelation as well. The Christ of the Apocalypse, like the Son of *Paradise Lost*, is both compassionate toward the faithful and unrelenting toward the enemies of God; the opening of the seals is a terrifying demonstration of the "wrath of the Lamb" (Rev. 6:16). A speech of the Father in Book 3 anticipates the appearance of Christ in triumph at the Last Judgment, and another in Book 10 pictures Sin and Death hurled into the mouth of hell by his "victorious Arm" (10. 634). His victory in Book 6 has been described by Joseph Summers as "an image and anticipation" of this final triumph.[17]

Certainly the spirit of the Son's victory over Satan is that of Revelation, particularly the nineteenth chapter, in which Christ appears on a white horse to judge and make war.[18] This conquering Christ has eyes like "a flame of

17. *The Muse's Method* (Cambridge, Mass., 1962), p. 135. John M. Steadman has said that the war in heaven is "the archetype of the Church's combats with her spiritual and temporal enemies on earth; Messiah's office as head and saviour of the angelic forces is the celestial paradigm of his role in human history, 'captain of our salvation.'" See *Milton and the Renaissance Hero* (Oxford, 1967), p. 94.

18. Revelation, 19:11–16:

> Then I saw heaven opened, and behold a white horse; and he that sat upon him was called Faithful and True, and in righteousness he doth judge and make war. His eyes were as a flame of fire, and on his head were many crowns; and he had a name written, that no man knew, but he himself. And he was clothed with a vesture dipped in blood: and his name is called The Word of God. And the armies which were in heaven followed

fire" (Milton's Christ gives off a "fierce Effusion . . . Of smoak and bickering flame, and sparkles dire" [6. 765–66] and with his armies casts Antichrist and his followers into the fiery lake. The warrior on a white horse of chapter six who goes forth with his bow, "conquering and to conquer," was identified with Christ by some commentators on Revelation,[19] and Revelation 6:1 was glossed occasionally by a reference to Psalm 45, the psalm that

---

> him upon white horses, clothed in fine linen, white and clean. And out of his mouth goeth a sharp sword, that with it he should smite the nations, and he will rule them with a rod of iron; and he treadeth the winepress of the fierceness and wrath of Almighty God. And he hath on his vesture and on his thigh a name written, King of Kings, and Lord of Lords.

This warrior "Faithful and True" is identified as Christ by modern commentators on Revelation (see Farrar, *The Revelation of St. John,* and Hans Lilje, *The Last Book of the Bible,* trans. Olive Wyon [Philadelphia, 1957]) and was widely understood as Christ in Renaissance commentaries. See Dent's *The Ruin of Rome* (London, 1603); Thomas Brightman's *A Revelation of the Revelation* (Amsterdam, 1615); John Napier's *A Plaine Discovery of the Whole Revelation of St. John* (London, 1611); William Cowper's *A Commentary Upon the Revelation,* in *Works* (London, 1623); and the influential work of David Pareus, admired by Milton, *A Commentary upon the Divine Revelation,* trans. Elias Arnold (Amsterdam, 1644). Pareus comments (p. 489): "The Majesticall description of the Captaine figureth the glorious comming of Christ from heaven, to judge Antichrist and the ungodly."

19. See Dent, Cowper, Pareus. Pareus's commentary on Christ's arrows provides an interesting example of how contrasting roles were reconciled. Literally, they are arrows piercing the enemies of God; allegorically, they represent the gospel piercing the souls of the godly. In *The Reason of Church Government* (CE, 3, pt. 1:269), Milton identifies the warrior of chapter 6 as the "Angell of the Gospell" in the course of arguing that the gospel is "the hidden might of Christ."

Milton drew upon for the instructions of the Father to the Son:

> *bring forth all my Warr,*
> *My Bow and Thunder, my Almightie Arms*
> *Gird on, and Sword upon thy puissant Thigh.*
>
> (6. 712–14)

The fact that Milton could take a passage from the forty-fifth psalm, actually an epithalamium for an unknown king, as a portrait of a militant Christ is a significant indication of the temper of protestant thought at the time.[20] In fact, the tenor of Protestant commentaries on Revelation in the sixteenth and seventeenth centuries helps to explain the military aspect of Milton's heaven and the harshness of Satan's defeat. Milton's thinking about the Son (at least about the third of the Son's three traditional roles of prophet, priest, and king)[21] was surely conditioned by the exultation of such commentators over the anticipated punishment of the pope and the Roman church, figured for them in the defeat of Antichrist and the destruction of Babylon. Writers of all shades of belief heralded the appearance of Christ as king and conqueror with a fierce joy in the victory of the true believers, regardless of when they expected this victory to come. From the nature of the Son's emergence as "Victorious King" (6. 886) it is evident that Milton was anticipating the second advent of Christ, "Arrayed in the glory and the power of the Father."[22] His execution of "fierce ven-

20. Broadbent points out that Milton misread the psalm, but his concern is with the irony that he sees in this misconception. See *Some Graver Subject,* p. 228.

21. See *Christian Doctrine,* CE, 15:287–303.

22. The phrase is a heading in *Christian Doctrine*. See CE, 16:355.

geance" (3. 399) is both a public justification of the Father's act of declaring him "universal King" (3. 317) and a foreshadowing of the end of the great struggle begun by Satan. Then Christ will appear in heaven "with his mighty angels," we are told in the Second Epistle to the Thessalonians, and destroy the wicked "with the brightness of his coming."[23]

Milton's emphasis on divine power implies the security of the angels and the saints whose arrival we anticipate. They are safe behind the battlements under the protection of God. But our sense of their bliss and repose depends strongly upon pastoral scenes that have little to do with the aspects of heaven that I have been describing. The first suggestion of a pastoral heaven occurs in the description of the rejoicing of the angels before the thrones of the Father and the newly elevated Son in Book 3. Milton explains that the "Immortal Amarant" of the angels' crowns was removed from Eden to heaven after the Fall:

> *There grows,*
> *And flours aloft shading the Fount of Life,*
> *And where the river of Bliss through midst of Heavn*
> *Rolls o're* Elisian *Flours her Amber stream.*
> (3. 355–59)

By the addition of flowers Milton makes the "river of the water of life" of Revelation the basis for a pleasant natural setting; we can almost see a surrounding meadow.

The description of the tree of life in Revelation confounds the imagination: "In the midst of the city street, on both sides of the river, was the tree of life, bearing

23. 2 Thessalonians, 1:7; 2:8.

twelve fruits." One can visualize this odd configuration of street, river, and tree only with difficulty. Milton offers a landscape instead of an emblem, showing the angels at rest "By living Streams among the Trees of Life" (5. 652). In his explanation of the nature of angelic food Raphael pictures an inviting natural world:

*In Heav'n the Trees*
*Of life ambrosial fruitage bear, and vines*
*Yield Nectar, though from off the boughs each Morn*
*We brush mellifluous Dewes, and find the ground*
*Cover'd with pearly grain.*

(5. 426–30)

If the "ambrosial fruitage" were described more concretely, it would lose its mystery, and Milton's heaven is meant to tease the imagination. It is enough like Eden to be comprehensible yet not fully knowable. We marvel, with Adam, at the daily miracle of "mellifluous Dewes" and "pearly grain."

The angelic banquet that Raphael describes threatens to become Homeric with its tables and cups of pearl, diamond, and "massie Gold" (5. 630), but by showing the angels "On flours repos'd, and with fresh flourets crownd" Milton anchored the scene in a pastoral heaven. We first see Adam and Eve "in the happie Garden plac't, / Reaping immortal fruits of joy and love" (3. 66–67). Here the angels "in communion sweet / Quaff immortalitie and joy" before the "all bounteous King," who rejoices in their joy.

In this way the act of eating or drinking is shown as a symbol of participation in the joy of paradise or heaven. But in Eden this joy is always a matter of sensuous pleasure. Milton can express the "enormous bliss" of Adam and Eve by groves of spices and a luxuriant nuptial bower. The dimly seen pastoral landscape of heaven is a way of suggesting a more highly refined bliss that depends not on the gratification of the senses but on the immediate presence of God.[24]

The angels eat "before" God and sleep under his "unsleeping eyes," enjoying a repose that we can only imagine as more complete than that of Adam and Eve in their Garden. The scene of sleeping angels in their tents "Fannd with Coole Winds" (5. 655) is the most important indication in the poem of the peace of heaven that "passeth understanding." This is the closest Milton comes to showing what it is to share in the "Holy Rest" (6. 272) of God. Waking or sleeping, the angels are not disturbed by the passions that threaten to disrupt the calm of Adam and Eve. As Satan, an obvious exception, gives in to his anger and pride, he appears distinctly more human and less angelic. The faithful angels enjoy a perfect equilibrium of the faculties that comes from the satisfaction of all desires. They exemplify the state that Augustine imagines the saints attain: "in that life necessity shall have no place, but full, certain, secure, everlasting felicity."[25] Even the mind is satisfied. For Dante, and surely for Milton as well, heaven contains the truth in which the intellect rests ("nel vero in che si queta ogni intelletto").[26]

24. Compare the ecstasy of the senses that Fletcher pictures:

*Here the glad soules the face of beauty kisse,*
*Powr'd out in pleasure, on their beds of blisse. . . .*
*Their braine sweet incense with fine breath accloyes.*
(*Poetical Works*, 1, 83)

25. *The City of God*, trans. Marcus Dods (New York, 1950), p. 864.

26. *Paradiso*, 28.

The repose of the angels in *Paradise Lost* is important partly because it foreshadows the "eternal paradise of rest" that man will reach after his wanderings in the world's wilderness. An emphasis on the sabbatical rest of the saints is a significant strain in Protestant thought, a corollary to the idea of constant spiritual warfare in this world.[27] Rest at the end of the pilgrimage of life is the "rest from their labours" promised in Revelation (14:13) to those who die in the Lord, the "saints' everlasting rest" that Richard Baxter saw as the goal of a Christian life. Milton defined it in *Christian Doctrine* as the "Sabbatical rest or eternal peace in heaven" of which earthly sabbaths are a "shadow."[28] Du Bartas had made the same point in more enthusiastic language:

> *He would, this Sabbath should a figure be*
> *Of the blest Sabbath of Eternity. . . .*
> *'Tis the grand* Jubilé, *Feast of all Feasts,*
> *Sabbath of Sabbaths, end-less Rest of Rests.*[29]

The conception of a pastoral heaven did not originate

27. See Calvin, *Institutes,* trans. John Allen (Philadelphia, 1936), 2:253: "Let us be content within these limits which God prescribes to us—that the souls of pious men, after finishing their laborious warfare, depart into a state of blessed rest, where they wait with joy and pleasure for the fruition of the promised glory."

28. *Christian Doctrine,* CE, 17:175.

29. *The Complete Works of Joshua Sylvester,* ed. A. B. Grosart (London, 1880), 1:104. *The Faerie Queene* ends with the contemplation of the "steadfast rest of all things, firmly stayed / Upon the pillars of eternity":

> *For all that moveth doth in change delight;*
> *But thenceforth all shall rest eternally*
> *With him that is the God of Sabaoth hight.*
> (*F.Q.,* 7.8.2.)

with Milton, of course; it is entwined with the tradition of the earthly paradise. Revelation provided the idea of a celestial paradise but not the substance, which owes more to Virgil. The same Christian writers who borrowed from Virgil in elaborating the earthly paradise took Elysium as a model for heaven. Bartlett Giamatti has pointed out that Dracontius, the fifth-century African poet, describes the celestial paradise in language that is quite close to Virgil's, picturing lawns, groves, and "sedesque beatas."[30] Prudentius, writing in the fourth century, offers in one of his hymns an alluring prospect of gardens with murmuring springs, spices, and such flowers as violets and crocuses:

*Here the souls of the blest wandering in grassy meads*
*Blend their voices in song, chanting melodious hymns*
*That devoutly resound through the happy glades,*
*And with radiant feet they tread the lilies fair.*[31]

In the medieval vision-literature sampled by Howard Rollins Patch, heaven usually appears as a meadow,[32] as

30. See *The Earthly Paradise in the Renaissance Epic* (Princeton, 1966), p. 66.

31. *The Poems of Prudentius,* trans. Sister M. Clement Eagen (Washington, 1962), I, 36 (*Cathemerinon,* 5, 113–24). Franz Cumont traces the evolution of pagan thought on the afterlife by which the abode of the blessed was transferred from the underworld to heaven. See *After Life in Roman Paganism* (New Haven, 1922), chap. 8.

32. In *The Other World* (Cambridge, Mass., 1950). A. B. Van Os, in *Religious Visions* (Amsterdam, 1932), p. 21, offers the following characterization of medieval visions of heaven: "Heaven is mostly represented as a meadow with fragrant flowers, where the elected are enjoying themselves with sports, dancing, singing, and looking upon God. As a rule they are dressed in white, adorned with gold ornaments and precious stones."

in the description of heaven from the *Vision of Drythelm,* quoted by Bede (and thus probably familiar to Milton):

> And behold there was there a very broad and pleasant field . . . full of the fragrance of fresh flourishing flowers. . . . Here is a fair light, gatherings of men in white garments, and the melodious noise of musicians.[33]

The Elysian heaven of Milton's Latin elegy on Lancelot Andrewes is an unusually rich vision of this sort, in which details from Revelation blend with echoes of Ovid and Virgil. Angels welcome the great preacher to flowery fields, silver rivers, fragrant breezes, and shady places formed by vines. Milton emphasizes the radiance of the place, which recalls the "camposque nitentis" of Virgil's Elysium, and the wonder and pleasure that the landscape evokes. Only the fact that his singers have wings and harps, and invite Andrewes to rest from his labors, identifies the scene as heaven.

Heaven is both city and paradise in medieval hymns on the joys of the New Jerusalem such as Peter Damian's "Ad perennis vitae fontem meus sitit nunc arida," Hildebert's "Me receptet Sion illa," and Bernard of Cluny's "Urbs Sion aurea."[34] Bernard's use of earthly paradise

33. Bede, *Ecclesiastical History,* trans. J. E. King (London and New York, 1930), 2:261.

34. See *The Oxford Book of Medieval Latin Verse,* ed. F. J. E. Raby (Oxford, 1959), pp. 187, 222, 224. Stanley Stewart, commenting on the presence of garden elements in descriptions of heaven, cites a similar hymn of Augustine translated by Sylvester. See *The Enclosed Garden* (Madison, Wis., 1966), p. 212. Stewart notes that heaven frequently was made to resemble the Garden of Eden in the longer allegorical poems of the seventeenth century, for example, Thomas Peyton's *The Glasse of Time* (1620).

motifs to mirror the undying joys of the blessed is typical:

> *Pax ibi florida, pascua vivida, viva medulla;*
> *Nulla molestia, nulla tragoedia, lacrima nulla.*[35]

In the Renaissance the tradition of a celestial paradise was transmitted primarily by the *consolatio* of the pastoral elegy. Behind the pastoral heaven in which the resurrected Lycidas finds his home, "Where other groves, and other streams along, / With *Nectar* pure his oozy Lock's he laves," are such poems as the fifth eclogue from Sannazzaro's *Arcadia* and Ronsard's first eclogue, noted as possible sources by Milton's editors:

> *Altri monti, altri piani,*
> *Altri boschecti et rivi*
> *Vedi nel cielo et più novelli fiori,*
> *Altri Fauni et Silvani*
> *Per luoghi dolci estivi*
> *Seguir le Nymphe in più felici amori.*[36]

> *Tu vois autres forests, tu vois autres riuages.*
> *Autres plus hauts rochers, autres plus verds bocages,*
> *Autres prez plus herbus & ton troupeau tu pais*
> *D'autres plus belles fleurs qui ne meurent jamais.*[37]

35. Peace is blossoming there, the pastures are green, the sap is living; there is no trouble, no tragedy, no weeping.

36. Other mountains, other plains, other woods and streams thou beholdest in heaven, and fresher flowers and other Fauns and Silvani in sweet places of summer's warmth, following the nymphs in happier loves.

37. Thou beholdest other forests, other shores, other higher rocks, other greener groves, other grassier meadows, and thou pasturest thy flocks with other fairer flowers that never die. Translations in nn. 36 and 37 by Harry Joshua Leon, in *The Pastoral Elegy,* ed. Thomas Perrin Harrison (Austin, Texas, 1939).

Visions of this sort often represent a curious fusion of Arcadia and Elysium (or the traditional earthly paradise). Sometimes this hybrid celestial paradise verges on the ludicrous, as in Boccaccio's "Olympia" eclogue, where the elders of Revelation become satyrs and an aged shepherd sits with the Lamb on his lap. Yet such a heaven can offer a kind of consolation that a golden New Jerusalem cannot, simply because it links the bliss of heaven with the emotions called up by an idealized pastoral world. If the celestial paradise has flowers and streams and one can enjoy there an unbroken concord with nature and with one's companions, then it seems a perfected version of our own world. The greenness of heaven ("The feeldes ay fresh, the grasse ay greene")[38] promises that life and pleasure will be renewed continually there.

The consolation of the pastoral elegy typically promises the restoration of harmony between man and an idealized natural world that has been brutally interrupted by death. The blight that death brings upon the landscape in the pastoral elegy is both a sign of nature's mourning and a reminder of the change that nothing in nature can escape. Although the canker and the frost of *Lycidas,* and the weeds and rotting corn of *Epitaphium Damonis,* appear to be unnatural reactions to death, they are in fact thoroughly natural phenomena. With the collapse of the pastoral fiction, reality breaks in on the poet, forcing the recognition that decay and disorder are a part of life. The equilibrium thus lost can be recovered if the fiction of a pastoral world is superseded by a higher fiction of a pastoral heaven beyond the possibility of change.

38. Spenser, imitating Marot, in the November eclogue from *The Shepheardes Calender.*

In both *Lycidas* and *Paradise Lost* celestial groves and streams make the pleasures of heaven seem to resemble those that we already know, but these pleasures are overshadowed by the more solemn, spiritual joys arising from the praise of God and the fellowship of the saints. In neither poem do classical and Christian elements casually mingle as they do in Spenser's description of Dido in a heavenly Elysium ("She raignes a goddesse now emong the saintes"). Milton's vision of heaven came to be dominated by the high festivities pictured in Revelation. The Elysian landscape, described in enthusiastic detail in *Elegy III*, yields in importance in *Lycidas* to the "solemn troops, and sweet Societies" that welcome Edward King. Yet the two lines (174–75) of groves, streams, and nectar establish an image of perfected nature and paradisal joy. Two lines are enough, just as several shadowy scenes are enough to suggest a pastoral heaven in *Paradise Lost*. By leaving these scenes indistinct Milton could suggest that the joys Adam will find in a heavenly paradise will resemble those of Eden and yet transcend them. A more fully described pastoral heaven, such as that of Boccaccio or Marot, may promise little more than earthly joys.

Milton found various ways of insisting on the correspondence between his heavenly and earthly paradises while at the same time differentiating them. The crowns of the angels are "inwove with Amarant and Gold" (3. 352) instead of simply golden. The pavement that shines "like a Sea of Jasper" is "Impurpl'd with Celestial Roses" (3. 365). By such a balancing of natural and artificial elements Milton fused the celestial paradise and the New Jerusalem, softening the image of the holy city. Yet the fact that the "Elisian" flowers of heaven are "unfading," not subject to decay under any conditions, reminds us that the beauty of Eden's flowers (such as the mosaic of iris, roses, and jessamin, violet, crocus, and hyacinth that adorns the nuptial bower) is vulnerable. Fragrance in heaven is "ambrosial fragrance" from the mouth of God, a reminder of Eden and also of Eden's distance from the source of highest bliss. The epithets "ambrosial," "Elisian," and "amaranthin" all work to transmute the earthly paradise into a purer celestial paradise, an environment that nourishes the life of the soul rather than that of the senses.

The paradisal aspect of heaven suggests only part of the bliss enjoyed by the angels. To the satisfaction of repose Milton added the greater fulfillment of active attendance upon God. In his portrayal of life in heaven Milton alternated between images of service and of rest. From one scene it appears that the life of the angels is spent in singing hymns before the throne, while from others it seems that feasting, or resting in bowers, is the rule. These two aspects of celestial life do not appear contradictory in Milton's heaven, but for others the idea of a sabbatical rest required some qualification. Donne virtually explained it away. After observing, with characteristic amplification, that the saints of God have no rest in this life because it is "a businesse, and a perplext businesse, a warfare, and a bloody warfare, a voyage, and a tempestuous voyage," he argued:

> If we understand this rest to be a Cessation, Intermission, the Saints in heaven have none of that, in thir service. It is a labour that never wearies, to serve God there.[39]

And Richard Baxter concluded that the everlasting rest of the saints "containeth a sweet and constant action of all

39. *Sermons,* 8:52.

the powers of the soul and body" in the "fruition" of God. For him it was a "rest without rest," such as that of the "four living creatures" of the fourth chapter of Revelation who "rest not day nor night" but continually praise God.[40] This rest may be understood, then, as a release from the active warfare of this life and a profound inner peace, but not as a cessation of activity. Milton's angels, like Baxter's saints, can be said to enjoy a paradoxical "rest without rest" in heaven.

The angels of *Paradise Lost* serve God as messengers and as soldiers, but the highest and most satisfying form of celestial service is the praise of God. Heaven rings with the hallelujahs of angelic choirs. With sacred song they celebrate the anointing of the Son, the defeat of Satan, the days of Creation: all the occasions for "Jubilee." Milton implies that the activity of praise never completely ceases in heaven. Some of the angels "alternate" hymns about the throne of God all night long, Raphael informs Adam (5. 656–57). In their morning hymn Adam and Eve imagine the angels' praise of God to be continuous:

*Speak yee who best can tell, ye Sons of Light.*
*Angels, for yee behold him, and with songs*
*And choral symphonies, Day without Night,*
*Circle his Throne rejoycing, yee in Heav'n.*
(5. 160–63)

40. See *The Saints Everlasting Rest* (London, 1649), p. 28. See also Ulrich Simon, *Heaven in the Christian Tradition* (New York, 1958), pp. 233–36. Simon traces the concept of the sabbatical rest in the Bible and rabbinical commentary. From New Testament texts he understands the heavenly Sabbath as a "continual feast day": "The participants are released from the burden of toil so as to be free for the worship of God" (p. 236). Compare Augustine's formula for describing the various aspects of life in heaven: "There we shall rest and see, see and love, love and praise" (*The City of God,* p. 867).

For Milton the beatific vision necessarily involves praise; the saints will circle the throne singing their "Hymns of high praise" (6. 745), joining the angels in celebrating God's power and mercy. In *Christian Doctrine* Milton quotes the sixtieth psalm to illustrate the happiness that arises from seeing God face to face: "in thy presence is fulness of joy; at thy right hand there are pleasures for evermore." The evidence of *Paradise Lost* suggests that this fullness of joy naturally finds expression in praise and that such praise is to be thought of as communal rather than individual. The angels act as one in expressing their love of God, especially in times of special rejoicing, when "no voice but well could joine / Melodious part, such concord is in Heav'n" (3. 369–70).

Although Milton distinguishes orders of angels and allows personalities to emerge during the crisis in heaven (Abdiel's case is an extreme example of the necessity for moral choice), individual differences disappear in the harmony before God. If the angels do not show the contempt of self that Augustine associates with the city of God, they at least seem to lose all consciousness of self in praise. The regularity of their motions, whether they move in circles or in "Mystical dance," is not only a sign of the order of the universe but proof of their selflessness in submitting to this order. Where the fallen angels often move erratically, with sudden eruptions of energy (building Pandaemonium, clashing in debate, exploring the terrain of hell), the inhabitants of heaven in their worship wheel and turn in patterns that suggest a perfect conformity to the will of God.

The heavenly harmony of angel choirs is at the heart of Milton's vision of heaven. Milton had to rely on the images of divine splendor that Revelation gave him to indicate the brilliance of God's courts. He could suggest the delights of pastoral repose through hints of a celestial paradise that man would eventually attain. But the promise of celestial bliss is most intensely realized in the scenes of celebration. The great choruses of Revelation had previously stirred Milton's imagination, with the most striking results in "At a Solemn Music," which recreates

> *That undisturbed Song of pure content,*
> *Ay sung before the saphire-colour'd throne*
> *To him that sits thereon*
> *With Saintly shout, and solemn Jubily,*
> *Where the bright Seraphim in burning row*
> *Their loud up-lifted Angel trumpets blow,*
> *And the Cherubick host in thousand quires*
> *Touch their immortal Harps of golden wires,*
> *With those just Spirits that wear victorious Palms,*
> *Hymns devout and holy Psalms*
> *Singing everlastingly.*

For Milton the supreme joy of heaven was that of joining in the song of the "celestial consort." To do so is to join, as he imagined Edward King and Charles Diodati joining, the communion of the blessed and through perfect harmony to come as close as one ever can to union with God. The dominant mood of heaven is festive, in keeping with Milton's view of dynamic communal praise as the highest expression of the love of God.

The paleness of Milton's heaven beside his richly colored Eden aptly illustrates Wallace Stevens' dictum: "Death is the mother of beauty." The ripeness of Eden's beauty affects us because we know that paradise is about to admit the "change of death" and become a part of "our perishing earth."[41] Better crocuses and jessamin than amaranthus, roses that fade than unfading and undescribed "Elisian" flowers, we may well say. It is difficult for most of us to respond to the "blessed vision" of God or the joy of unceasing praise, especially when these satisfactions are juxtaposed to the enormously engaging drama of Adam and Eve. The vicissitudes of "our first Parents," and even the pageant of human history revealed by Michael in the last two books, inevitably have a stronger appeal than the unchanging reality of heaven, but heaven is the theological if not the dramatic center of the poem, the image of the true city and the true paradise toward which the action of the human drama moves. In the perspective of God, which Milton repeatedly invites us to assume, past, present, and future time are framed by eternity. One of the lessons of the poem is that we should fix our vision on heaven and not on the illusory power and splendor of the world or, with a nostalgic backward glance, on the lost bliss of Eden. For heaven is not simply one level of Milton's cosmic stage in *Paradise Lost* but the only stable element in his universe. It will remain, "firmly stayed / Upon the pillars of eternity," when the rest is gone.

41. These phrases are also from Stevens's "Sunday Morning."

# 4

# THE PASTORAL DAY

Because Milton gave Adam and Eve work to do and delicately adjusted their activity to the rhythm of nature's changes, the bliss of paradise cannot be understood except in terms of the pattern of their daily activity. The constant repetition of this pattern, in harmony with the cyclical movement of the "Wheele / Of Day and Night," gives a sense of timelessness to life in the prelapsarian world. When all days are the same, the concept of mutability is meaningless. Yet within the day itself differences in time serve important dramatic functions. My concern here is with the routine of the individual day, which has received little critical attention, and with the significance that is attached to its disruption after the Fall.[1]

The well-defined pattern of life in the Garden is governed by the rising and falling of the sun. This pattern—

1. On the timelessness of life in the Garden, see Isabel Gamble MacCaffrey, *"Paradise Lost" as Myth* (Cambridge, Mass., 1959), pp. 73–75, and Anne Davidson Ferry, *Milton's Epic Voice* (Cambridge, Mass., 1963), especially p. 156. See also Joseph H. Summers, *The Muse's Method* (Cambridge, Mass., 1962), chap. 3, on the "Grateful vicissitude" of nature in Eden.

rising at dawn, taking refuge from the heat of the sun at noon, and retiring in the evening—owes little to the epic antecedents of *Paradise Lost* or to the various models that shaped Milton's conception of paradise, but descriptions of the three primary times of the day are commonplace in classical and Renaissance pastoral poetry. The basis for the convention is the routine of the shepherd's day, sensitively described by Virgil in his third Georgic:

*But when the west winds call and the exquisite warm*
*season*
*Ushers them out, both sheep and goats, to glade and*
*pasture,*
*At the first wink of the Morning Star let us wend away*
*To the frore fields, while the morning is young, the*
*meadow pearly,*
*And dew so dear to cattle lies on the tender grass. . . .*
*But now it's the noonday heat, make for a shady combe*
*Where some great ancient-hearted oak throws out its*
*huge*
*Boughs, or the wood is black with*
*A wealth of holm-oak and broods in its own haunted*
*shadow.*
*Then give them runnels of water again and let them*
*browse*
*About sundown, when the cool star of evening assuages*
*The air, and moonlight falls now with dew to freshen*
*the glades,*
*And the kingfisher's heard on the shore and the warbler*
*in woody thickets.*

(322–26, 331–38)[2]

2. *Eclogues and Georgics of Virgil,* trans. C. Day Lewis, Doubleday Anchor Book (Garden City, N.Y., 1964).

The fresh detail of this scene makes it seem real and immediate, yet the peacefulness and order that Virgil is able to suggest remind us of the ideal, timeless world of more stylized pastoral poetry. In the *Eclogues* Virgil uses descriptions of the coming of evening to show the calm that invariably returns to the pastoral world at the end of the day (the first and second close with lengthening shadows, the sixth and tenth with the coming of Hesperus). References to evening, and to morning and noon, are more frequent and usually more perfunctory in Renaissance pastoral poetry. Spenser ends all but two of the eclogues in *The Shepheardes Calender* with at least an oblique reference to evening. The "shepherd-swains" of Phineas Fletcher's *Purple Island* regulate their song by observing all three traditional periods of the day. The first canto ends at noon, the second at evening; the third, beginning again with "Morning fresh," ends at noon with the shepherds withdrawing to a glade to eat their "simple cates." However mechanical these references may become in Fletcher and his contemporaries, they serve as a way of defining the limits of the pastoral world and suggesting its essential harmony. As long as the rhythm of nature is observed, no quarrel, or love melancholy, or outburst of satirical invective can disrupt permanently the tranquillity of pastoral life; calm is normally restored with evening, and morning begins the cycle anew.

The mold was broken playfully by Marvell, whose Mower naïvely proclaims himself nature's favorite, only to be ruined by love:

> *I am the Mower* Damon, *known*
> *Through all the Meadows I have mown.*
> *On me the Morn her dew distills*

*Before her darling Daffadils.*
*And, if at Noon my toil me heat,*
*The Sun himself licks off my Sweat.*
*While, going home, the Ev'ning sweet*
*In cowslip-water bathes my feet.*
(41–48)[3]

In *Lycidas* Milton made a bolder use of the familiar time scheme. The leisurely days of the poet and Lycidas in the period of their innocence are measured by dawn, the "sultry horn" of the "Gray-fly," and the evening star. But this calm is destroyed, and the return to the rhythm of nature in the final lines of the poem (with the coming of evening and the promise of a new day) reflects a more complete peace based upon the fuller understanding at which the poet has arrived. As MacCaffrey has shown in her sensitive reading of the poem, the coda reveals a "new wisdom," which "understands the pastoral world for what it is—a foreshadowing, not an echo."[4]

In *Paradise Lost* the time scheme that is telescoped in *Lycidas* unfolds gradually.[5] The descriptions of times of the day, like passages of natural description, enlarge our sense of the innocence and bliss of Adam and Eve, and they establish the rhythm of daily activity that is dictated by nature and thus sanctified by God. Dawn renews the vitality of Adam and Eve and their delight in the Gar-

3. "Damon the Mower," *Poems of Andrew Marvell,* ed. Hugh Macdonald (Cambridge, Mass., 1963).

4. "*Lycidas:* The Poet in a Landscape," in *The Lyric and Dramatic Milton,* ed. Joseph H. Summers (New York, 1965), p. 90.

5. It is briefly sketched in the description of Mulciber's fall from heaven: "from Morn / To Noon he fell, from Noon to dewy Eve. / A Summers day" (I. 742–44).

den. The "sweet hour of Prime" (5. 170), the first hour of the day, is the time when Eden is at its freshest and most fragrant. The eagerness of Adam to proceed to his work on the one morning when Eve sleeps late can be taken as typical; it is an instinctive response to the quickening of nature:

*Awake*
*My fairest, my espous'd, my latest found,*
*Heav'ns last best gift, my ever new delight,*
*Awake, the morning shines, and the fresh field*
*Calls us, we lose the prime, to mark how spring*
*Our tended Plants. . . .*

(5. 17–22)

Dawn also means a renewal of communion with God:

*Now when as sacred Light began to dawne*
*In* Eden *on the humid Flours, that breathd*
*Thir morning incense, when all things that breath,*
*From th'Earths great Altar send up silent praise*
*To the Creator, and his Nostrils fill*
*With grateful Smell, forth came the human pair*
*And joind thir vocal Worship to the Quire*
*Of Creatures wanting voice, that done, partake*
*The season, prime for sweetest Sents and Aires.*

(9. 192–200)

Each day is like a new Creation, with all plants and creatures brought to life by the return of "sacred Light," as if by the touch of God. The fragrance of the flowers, released by the sun, becomes incense offered by earth to the Creator, a part of nature's contribution to the morning rites of Adam and Eve.

Milton had to depart from the traditional view of the earthly paradise as a place where there is no excessive heat to preserve the importance of noon in his time scheme.[6] God tells Raphael that he will find Adam in a bower "from the heat of Noon retir'd, / To respit his day-labour with repast, / Or with repose" (5. 231–33). Adam, greeting his visitor, invites him

*in yonder shadie Bowre*
*To rest, and what the Garden choicest bears*
*To sit and taste, till this meridian heat*
*Be over, and the Sun more coole decline.*
(5. 367–70)

On a day not graced with such a visit, this period of rest would simply be a natural, restorative pause at the mid-point of the day's activity and an unusually peaceful time in the Garden.

The repose at the conclusion of the day's work is naturally more complete than that of noon, and Milton gives the evening hour more attention. We first see Adam and Eve at the end of the day as they stroll hand in hand and then settle on a flowery bank to enjoy their "Supper Fruits" (4. 331) while the sun declines. This time of relaxation and general pleasure at the approach of "grateful Eevning milde" (4. 647) is the most appropriate hour for a tableau showing the frolicking of the animals about the "Lords" (4. 290) of nature. The peace of the Garden seems to deepen as evening comes and yields imperceptibly to night:

*Now came still Eevning on, and Twilight gray*
*Had in her sober Liverie all things clad;*
*Silence accompanied, for Beast and Bird,*

6. In most versions of the earthly paradise (including the false paradises of Ariosto, Tasso, and Spenser), the weather is said to be uniformly delightful, and the air is described as temperate or cool.

*They to thir grassie Couch, these to thir Nests*
*Were slunk, all but the wakeful Nightingale;*
*She all night long her amorous descant sung;*
*Silence was pleas'd: now glow'd the Firmament*
*With living Saphirs:* Hesperus *that led*
*The starrie Host, rode brightest, till the Moon*
*Rising in clouded Majestie, at length*
*Apparent Queen unvaild her peerless light,*
*And o're the dark her Silver Mantle threw.*
(4. 598–609)[7]

Heaven has its morning and evening (if not full night) for "change delectable" (5. 629), and the cycle of life in Eden is obviously meant to seem attuned to the pattern of angelic activity.[8] Milton's description of a celestial twilight in Book 5 (642–57)—the angels are "Fannd with coole Winds" as they sleep "By living Streams among the Trees of Life"—suggests that the repose of Adam and Eve before the Fall is at least comparable to the peace that is enjoyed in heaven. There is no real repose for the in-

7. This is another traditional type of *descriptio* of time, or *chronographia,* as Puttenham would call it. See Virgil's description óf night in the fourth book of the *Aeneid* (ed. F. A. Hirtzel [Oxford, 1950]):

*Nox erat et placidum carpebant fessa soporem*
*corpora per terras, silvaeque et saeva quierant*
*aequora, cum medio volvuntur sidera lapsu,*
*cum tacet omnis ager, pecudes pictaeque volucres,*
*quaeque lacus late liquidos quaeque aspera dumis*
*rura tenent, somno positae sub nocte silenti.*
(522–27)

8. The descriptions of dawn in heaven during the war of the angels have much the same function as descriptions of dawn in the *Iliad;* they separate the days of battle and mark the passage of time. But these days are atypical. The normal pattern is represented by the description of twilight in Book 5, which suggests the timelessness of a pastoral world.

habitants of hell; one of the greatest torments of the place is the complete absence of change in the environment. Since there is no "Grateful vicissitude" (6. 8), in fact, no way at all to mark the passage of time, there can be no natural rhythm to the activity of the fallen angels. It is appropriate that they are never shown asleep and that the only eating we see them do is a form of torture. Satan and his followers defy the lifeless world around them; they establish their empire over it and achieve what order they have by military discipline. Life in the fallen world, though it may be hard, at least has a natural order established by the alternation of day and night and the rotation of the seasons.

The rhythm of life in paradise is important primarily because of the dramatic significance that Milton gives to its disruption. Like all the aspects of the original state of Adam and Eve, the harmony of man with nature cannot be appreciated fully until it has been lost, that is, until we have vicariously experienced the fall from bliss of our "first Parents." But what is more remarkable about Milton's concern with the times of day in *Paradise Lost* is the subtlety with which he reveals the changed moral and emotional condition of Adam and Eve by showing them to be out of phase with nature's cycle after the Fall. Although there is no real disruption of the normal pattern of activity until Eve eats the fruit at noon on the fatal day, the impending upheaval is foreshadowed in interesting ways.

It is significant that Satan enters the Garden for the first time as evening is approaching. The effect of this timing is rather like that of the first stirrings of revolution in heaven. We see Satan whispering his plans for a rebellion to Beelzebub immediately after the angels are shown asleep in their "Pavilions numberless" (5. 653).

The discordant note seems harsher because it is introduced into an extraordinarily peaceful scene. One reason that Satan's "bold entrance" (4. 882) into the Garden is shocking is that it comes at the most tranquil hour of the day, a time of relaxation and special intimacy for Adam and Eve. A reference to the familiar world, "where Shepherds pen thir Flocks at eeve" (4. 185), reminds us that evening should be a time of security. But the point of the simile is to focus attention upon the "prowling Wolfe" (4. 183) that is about to enter the fold, and thus to serve notice that the security of the Garden is illusory.

When Ithuriel and Zephon apprehend Satan "at the eare of *Eve*" (4. 800), they find him in the place of greatest sanctity and privacy in the Garden, the nuptial bower. In denouncing Satan for his intrusion, Gabriel characterizes him as employed "to violate sleep, and those / Whose dwelling God hath planted here in bliss" (4. 883–84). The strong verb "violate" is particularly effective because it makes the initial effort to unsettle Eve more clearly a disturbance of the order of nature. Later, we see the effects of this violation of sleep in the disarray and confusion of Eve, whose looks are normally "more chearful and serene / Then when fair Morning first smiles on the World" (5. 123–24). The urgency of Adam's words ("Awake, the morning shines . . . / . . . we lose the prime" [5. 20–21]) is lost on her. Before she can do anything, she must relate the dream and find some explanation for it. This Adam confidently provides, dispelling doubts and kissing away tears, but the ease with which Eve recovers her assurance is ironic. The reader is left to ponder the implications of the dream, which are underscored by the fact that the day's activity has been interrupted; although the loss of equilibrium is temporary, and quickly remedied, it points to the more serious dislocation that is to follow.

The Fall itself occurs at noon. Various theories have been advanced to explain Milton's choice of this time, the most interesting one by Jackson Cope, who has attempted to trace it to the influence of exegetical commentary on Psalm 91:6, in which the psalmist promises protection from "the destruction that wasteth at noonday," or, in the language of the Vulgate, the "daemonio meridiano."[9]

9. *The Metaphoric Structure of "Paradise Lost"* (Baltimore, 1962), pp. 130–37. See also Grant McColley, *"Paradise Lost": An Account of Its Growth and Major Origins* (Chicago, 1940), p. 161, and Maurice Kelley, *This Great Argument* (Princeton, 1941), p. 148. McColley traces Milton's choice of noon to a desire to link the Fall with the darkness at noon on the day of the crucifixion, and Kelley argues that Milton's timing makes gluttony more clearly a part of Eve's sin. See also Albert R. Cirillo, "Noon-Midnight and the Temporal Structure of *Paradise Lost,*" *English Literary History* 29 (1962):372–95. Cirillo's argument depends upon the dubious assumption—which Cope seems to share—that every mention of noon in the poem is related to Eve's sin, including the reference to noon in the description of Mulciber's fall (1. 743). It should be said that noon and midnight were two of the few traditional times of the day available to Milton for dramatic purposes (others are dawn, prime, and sunset or evening). It is dramatically fitting that Satan on Niphates should address the sun when it is in its "Meridian Towre" (4. 30). And it is predictable, indeed almost inevitable, that if a specific time is to be given for the revolt in heaven and Satan's return to the Garden, it should be midnight. On the noonday demon, see Rudolph Arbesmann, "The 'Daemonium Meridianum' and Greek and Latin Patristic Exegesis," *Traditio* 14 (1958):17–31, and Roger Caillois, "Les démons de midi," *Revue de l'Histoire des Religions* 115 (1937):142–73, 116 (1937):54–83, 143–86. Cirillo, following the lead of Cope—for whom Satan is "the literal embodiment of the *daemonio meridiano*" (p. 136)—cites many of the traditional beliefs about the noon hour collected by Caillois in an effort to make Satan into a noonday demon. Caillois demonstrates that the middle of the day was associated with some religious observances, communication with the dead, apparitions,

Cope shows that Augustine and others (including Jeremy Taylor, who speaks of acting scenes of darkness in the face of the sun) identified deliberate sin with the day, and he cites several Old Testament references (Deut. 28:28–29, Job 5:14, Is. 59:10) to groping or stumbling at noon, understood to be the time of greatest light. According to Isaiah, "we stumble at noonday as in the night" because of sin. By having Eve yield to Satan's argument in full daylight, Milton emphasizes the fact that she sins consciously, contrasting the actual deed with the dream that foreshadowed it.[10]

---

sudden physical and mental afflictions, and erotic dreams, among other things. In medieval Christian tradition, the time came to be associated with *acedia,* which might give birth to other sins, including *luxuria.* Encounters with supernatural beings often occur at this time (Actaeon's discovery of Diana bathing, the appearance of the hippocentaur to St. Anthony).

What Cirillo fails to point out is that, although noon could be precisely defined as the time when the sun was in its zenith and shadows were shortest, it was commonly thought of in a more indefinite sense. The beliefs that Caillois assembles were associated with the period of greatest heat in the middle of the day (to which the term "noonday" refers), the time of siesta in the Mediterranean countries, or what we would call early afternoon. When Milton has Eve make her decision to eat the fruit as "the hour of Noon drew on" (9. 739), that is, as it approached, he places the Fall at about twelve o'clock, by which time she would have returned to meet Adam and prepare their meal. In other words, the Fall occurs just at the beginning of what is normally the time of "Noontide repast, or Afternoons repose" (9. 403), the period that corresponds to the time of retirement in the middle of the day, the dangers of which Caillois documents. Satan actually appears to Eve well before noon on the day of the Fall.

10. It should be noted that Milton makes no reference to the sun in connection with the noon of Eve's sin. In his treatment of the temptation there is none of the play on light and darkness normally associated with the conception of noon as

Yet the primary reason for Milton's choice of noon, I think, is the most obvious one, the dramatic appropriateness of this time in view of its importance in the life of Adam and Eve. Milton gives considerable emphasis to Eve's promise to return by noon, reminding us of the peacefulness of the hour and then, with powerful irony, looking ahead to the implications of Eve's failure to keep her promise:

> *Oft he to her his charge of quick returne*
> *Repeated, shee to him as oft engag'd*
> *To be returnd by Noon amid the Bowre,*
> *And all things in best order to invite*
> *Noontide repast, or Afternoons repose.*
> *O much deceav'd, much failing, hapless* Eve,
> *Of thy presum'd return! event perverse!*
> *Thou never from that houre in Paradise*
> *Foundst either sweet repast, or sound repose.*
> (9. 399–407)

The flowering of Eve's pride in the temptation scene has been prepared for by previous indications of her vanity. The final warning is her insistence upon working alone. It is interesting that the first argument she offers Adam is based upon efficiency; they will accomplish more separately, free from distraction. Adam's "mild answer" (9. 226), that their work was intended to be delightful and that it will keep the Garden orderly enough for their use, reflects a superior understanding of the purpose of

---

a time of sin. While it seems clear that Milton intended to associate deliberate sin with the day, it is difficult to be sure that his choice of noon was influenced by the tradition that Cope describes.

their daily routine.[11] For him it is a pledge of obedience and of contentment with the delights of the Garden. To violate the routine, as Eve does by altering the pattern of working with Adam, is to question God's plan and allow the will a dangerous latitude. Eve's demand for independence prepares us for her second, more serious violation of the routine, her failure to return by noon. Milton traces the growth of Eve's self-awareness by showing her increasing lack of concern for subordinating her activity to an unquestioned routine. Her supreme act of self-assertion is more clearly a sin against the order of nature because it comes at a time when the rhythm of the day demands a suspension of activity, a period of mental and physical relaxation. The unanticipated effect of Eve's indulgence of her pride is that her life and Adam's are thrown into confusion.

On the day of the Fall, the midday rest is completely transfigured. There is repose, after lovemaking (at an improper time and in an improper place), but it is a troubled sleep that is more like "unrest" (9. 1052). And although the fruit serves as the midday meal for Adam as well as Eve, this meal is a parody of the "sweet repast" that they normally enjoy at noon, if we can judge the typical meal by the one that they share with Raphael. The contrasts between the day of Raphael's visit and the

11. An incident in Book 4 points to a difference between Eve's sense of routine and Adam's. For Adam, the coming of evening is a signal that it is time to retire: "as Nature wills, Night bids us rest" (633). For Eve, it is an occasion for expressing her delight in the Garden, and her love: "With thee conversing I forget all time, / All seasons and thir change, all please alike" (639–40). Although Eve seems inclined to linger and enjoy the beauty of the evening, she graciously yields to Adam's judgment.

day of the Fall do a great deal to justify Milton's timing of Eve's sin. On the earlier day, Adam and Eve display a social poise and an instinctive formality that suit the occasion perfectly. Since Adam's "Nourisher" provides for his intellectual as well as his physical well-being, the leisurely meal is followed by a lecture. The language in which Adam describes his delight in Raphael's conversation makes learning seem as natural for him as eating, and more refreshing:

> *And sweeter thy discouse is to my eare*
> *Then Fruits of Palm-tree pleasantest to thirst*
> *And hunger both, from labour, at the houre*
> *Of sweet repast. . . .*
>
> (8. 211–14)

Raphael tells Adam that "Knowledge is as food, and needs no less / Her Temperance over Appetite" (7. 126–27). In the temptation scene the simile is inverted, with a kind of grim irony, as food becomes the means to knowledge. There is a shocking vulgarity about the way in which Eve gorges herself on the fruit; we are meant to recall the earlier scene in which she ministered gracefully to Raphael.

Adam and Eve spend the afternoon in "fruitless hours" of quarreling (9. 1188) until they are interrupted by the arrival of the Son of God at evening. By expanding the reference to God's coming "in the cool of the day" (Gen. 3:8) into a rich descriptive passage, Milton suggests that his "mild Judge" is as gentle as the approach of evening, and at the same time reveals the isolation of Adam and Eve in their shame and fear. They have cut themselves off from God and from the solace of nature:

> *Now was the Sun in Western cadence low*

*From Noon, and gentle Aires due at thir hour*
*To fan the Earth now wak'd, and usher in*
*The Eevning coole when he from wrauth more coole*
*Came the mild Judge and Intercessor both*
*To sentence Man: the voice of God they heard*
*Now walking in the Garden, by soft windes*
*Brought to thir Ears, while day declin'd, they heard,*
*And from his presence hid themselves among*
*The thickest Trees, both Man and Wife. . . .*
(10. 92–101)

For a moment, time seems to be suspended ("the voice of God they heard / . . . by soft windes / Brought to thir Ears, while day declin'd, they heard"); then the spell of evening is broken as the verse accelerates. The impersonal biblical phrase, "Man and Wife," effectively indicates the diminished stature of Adam and Eve. This vivid description of the evening serves much the same purpose as the brief sketch of the couch of flowers upon which Adam and Eve satisfy their lust; it makes us acutely conscious of what has been lost. Repose has given way to "shame, and perturbation, and despair, / Anger, and obstinacie, and hate, and guile" (10. 113–14).

The night brings no rest. It has become a time of "damps and dreadful gloom" (10. 848)—there is naturally no mention of the stars, or of the sounds of nightingales and angels—and serves as a fitting backdrop for Adam's lamentations. Dawn brings the same freshness to the Garden as before, and it finds Adam and Eve, now reconciled, stretched out on the ground asking forgiveness with sighs and tears. Inevitably, the scene recalls earlier dawns in Eden and especially the morning hymn. At the same time, the description of this dawn, when the "first fruits" of repentance spring from God's "implanted Grace" (11. 22–23), reflects the birth of hope in Adam and Eve:[12]

> *Meanwhile*
> *To resalute the World with sacred Light*
> Leucothea *wak'd, and with fresh dews imbalmd*
> *The Earth, when* Adam *and first Matron* Eve
> *Had ended now thir Orisons, and found*
> *Strength added from above, new hope to spring*
> *Out of despaire, joy, but with fear yet linkt.*
> (11. 133–39)

The tentative expectations of this difficult beginning are replaced, in Adam at least, by delight at the prospect of the glorious resurrection described by Michael:

> *Death over him no power*
> *Shall long usurp; ere the third dawning light*
> *Returne, the Starres of Morn shall see him rise*
> *Out of his grave, fresh as the dawning light. . . .*
> (12. 420–23)

Milton's final use of dawn in *Paradise Lost* looks forward to man's eventual triumph over death through

12. This scene may have been suggested by Tasso's more elaborate description of the dawn in *Jerusalem Delivered* (translated by Edward Fairfax [New York, 1963], p. 360), that answers Rinaldo's prayer for forgiveness on Mount Olivet:

> *Thus prayed he. With purple wings up flew,*
> *In golden weed, the morning's lusty queen,*
> *Begilding, with the radiant beams she threw,*
> *His helm, his harness, and the mountain green:*
> *Upon his breast and forehead gently blew*
> *The air, that balm and nardus breath'd unseen;*
> *And o'er his head, let down from clearest skies,*
> *A cloud of pure and precious dew there flies.*
> (18. 15)

Christ's victory; Adam and Eve, however, are still a long way from an understanding of their future at the beginning of the new day in Eden. The weariness reflected in Eve's suggestion to Adam that they resume their work, so unlike his invitation to her at the beginning of Book 5, reminds us again that they clash with their surroundings:

*But the Field*
*To labour calls us now with sweat impos'd,*
*Though after sleepless Night; for see the Morn,*
*All unconcern'd with our unrest, begins*
*Her rosie progress smiling; let us forth,*
*I never from thy side henceforth to stray,*
*Wherere our days work lies, though now enjoind*
*Laborious, till day droop; while here we dwell,*
*What can be toilsom in these pleasant Walkes?*
(11. 171–79)

The custom of rising at dawn and retiring at evening may be reestablished in another, "lower" world, where day can indeed "droop." But it is impossible for Adam and Eve to recover the perfect harmony with nature and with God that was a basic condition of their bliss. Instead, they must adjust to an unpredictable and seemingly hostile nature.

The eclipse announcing Michael's arrival, an interruption of the progress of the day that would not have been possible before the Fall, is an appropriate reminder that the procession of uniformly delightful days has ended for Adam and Eve. The last day in the Garden is given over to the solemn business of preparing Adam for the ordinary existence he must begin. If his introduction to the flux of history is inevitably bewildering, at least he is left with the assurance that the ordeal of human life will be succeeded by an eternity of bliss, in the "Ages of endless date" (12. 549) prophesied by Michael.

Adam's contemplation of eternity is brought to an abrupt end by Michael's comment that the "hour precise" (12. 589) demands his departure from the Garden. Although there is no exact indication of the time, the comparison of the advancing cherubim to "Ev'ning Mist" (12. 629) and the reference of the necessity of finding a place of rest suggest that evening is at hand.[13] There is a good reason for Milton's failure to indicate the hour by any of the usual means: these would suggest the repose normally associated with evening in the Garden. On this evening Adam and Eve show none of the fear that they displayed when the Son came in judgment, but they are not tranquil either. Though Adam knows that ultimately man will come to an "eternal Paradise of rest" (12. 314), he cannot be sure where he and Eve will rest for the night. The conclusion of *Paradise Lost,* which is often called quiet, is actually quite unlike the quiet close of a Virgilian eclogue. There is no feeling of completion, no perfect calm; we sense the uncertainty of the immediate future for Adam and Eve as they set out:

> *The World was all before them, where to choose*
> *Thir place of rest, and Providence thir guide:*
> *They hand in hand with wandring steps and slow,*
> *Through* Eden *took thir solitarie way.*
>
> (12. 646–49)

13. It might be objected that this view does not allow for the noon meal, but it seems improbable that Milton thought of Adam's vision as occupying only the morning. The omission of the customary midday repose can in fact be taken as another indication of the disorder brought into the life of Adam and Eve by the Fall.

It has been shown that Milton's conclusion is decidedly more optimistic than traditional renderings of the expulsion.[14] Certainly the grounds for hope—the possibilities that the world offers Adam and Eve, their mature love, the fact that they have "Providence" for a guide—are of extreme importance. But neither these encouraging signs nor the fact that Adam is consoled by his new understanding of the working of providence in history diminishes the somberness of the occasion.

F. T. Prince concludes his essay on the last two books of *Paradise Lost* with the observation that Milton's reference to the laborer "Homeward returning" is a "moving evocation of the life of toil and poverty and weariness and also of homely satisfactions—all the common experience of humanity—which Adam and Eve must now undertake."[15] I would add the qualification that one is not so conscious of homely satisfactions as of the threatening nature of the mist at the laborer's heel:

*and from the other Hill*
*To thir fixt Station, all in bright array*
*The Cherubim descended; on the ground*
*Gliding meteorous, as Ev'ning Mist*
*Ris'n from a River o're the marish glides,*
*And gathers ground fast at the Labourers heel*
*Homeward returning.*

(12. 626–32)

14. See Dick Taylor, Jr., "Milton's Treatment of the Judgment and the Expulsion in *Paradise Lost*," *Tulane Studies in English* 10 (1960):51–82, and Merritt Y. Hughes, "Some Illustrators of Milton: The Expulsion from Paradise," *Journal of English and Germanic Philology* 60 (1961):670–79.

15. "On the Last Two Books of *Paradise Lost*," *Essays and Studies* 11 (1958):52.

The special character of the simile is more obvious if it is set alongside a conventional statement of the theme of the return from labor, such as that of Virgil in his second Eclogue: "Look, ploughs feather the ground as the ox-teams draw them home, / And a declining sun enlarges the lengthening shadows" (66–67). There is no such peacefulness in the evening scene suggested by Milton's simile, in which the ominous mist takes the place of shadows or evening star. In the actual scene at the gate of Paradise, the flaming "Sword of God" (12. 633) bars Adam and Eve from the pastoral world where they knew true repose, forcing them into an unfamiliar setting where rest can be no more than temporary relief from hard labor, and perhaps from anxiety.

The openness of the conclusion of *Paradise Lost* makes it radically different from the conclusions of Milton's other major works. In *Paradise Regained* Christ's quiet return to his mother's house marks the completion of an important phase in his life and the resolution of doubts about his mission. The physical rest that awaits him reflects his inner peace. In *Samson Agonistes* emotional turbulence leads to catharsis, the "calm of mind, all passion spent" that the reader shares with Manoa and the chorus. The contrast with the conclusion of *Lycidas* is even more striking, because Milton restores the rhythm of nature in the concluding lines of that poem, suggesting by one last image of the pastoral world the peace that arises from the vision of Lycidas in heaven.

The final lines of *Paradise Lost* owe their extraordinary power to the fact that the rhythm of nature is not restored. We are engaged by the situation of Adam and Eve because repose has not yet been found, passions have not subsided completely. At the beginning of their journey through the world's wilderness, we are much closer to them—in their uncertainty and their human frailty—than to Christ, or an Old Testament hero, or a fictional shepherd singer, or the shadowy Venus and Adonis whom we see enjoying their luxurious repose in the epilogue of *Comus*. The knowledge that they have "Providence" for a guide, however reassuring this may be, does not relieve Adam and Eve of the burden of choice or make the plain seem any more hospitable, since they must learn to recognize and accept this providence in their lives. We can be certain that trials of faith and endurance lie ahead. As surely as Milton knew the supreme importance of patience, he knew that it is a virtue not easily won.

# 5

# FAIREST OF CREATION

Most contemporary discussion of Milton's Eve has concerned itself with the problems surrounding her sin: how she can sin if she is truly innocent, how Milton foreshadows her act, how Satan exploits the weaknesses that he discovers in her. It is a rare critic who does not touch on the narcissism of Eve's fascination with her image in the lake and the susceptibility to sin revealed by her dream of eating the fruit. Such psychological concern with Eve's flaws, though justified by the poem, is peculiarly modern. The danger of approaching Eve solely as a character in a drama whose human weaknesses can be spotted early by an alert reader is that we will fail to see how complex and engaging a figure she actually is. If it were not for the extraordinary interest of the action itself, Eve would strike us as an uncommonly simple character. She has none of the mystery of Lady Macbeth or even of Ophelia. Indeed, she has no secrets at all, even from Adam, to whom she is as transparent after the Fall as before.

Taking advantage of the larger freedom of the epic, Milton surrounded Eve with an aura that gives her a significance beyond that of a character in any ordinary drama. In her innocence she seems less a woman than a goddess-like figure of unparalleled grace and beauty, "Fairest of Creation." After eating the fruit she undergoes a transformation from majesty to simple humanity that suggests an Ovidian metamorphosis in reverse. Unlike Proserpina, whom she resembles in her loveliness and vulnerability, Eve falls into a world of death and sin. The great irony of her situation is that God's preeminent gift of beauty causes her ruin and Adam's. In entertaining Satan's flattery of her "Celestial Beauty" Eve forgets the first lesson she learned:

> *How beauty is excelld by manly grace*
> *And wisdom, which alone is truly fair.*
> (4. 490–91)

When Adam yields to Eve's charm against his better judgment and eats the fruit, he confirms his weakness before "Beauties powerful glance" (8. 533).[1]

To appreciate Eve's "perfect beauty" and the grace that enhances it, one must grasp her mythical dimension. Milton used description, commentary, and allusions not so much to characterize Eve as to persuade the reader of her special state of being. Repeated epithets such as "fair" and "lovely," and tableaux in which we see her either with Adam or alone fix our impression of Eve's perfection and hold the threat of mutability at bay. Allusions, especially, seem to remove Eve from the flux of merely human experience; the qualities of a Venus or a Diana are constant. Milton's intricate web of allusions

1. For a fuller discussion of the role of Eve's beauty in the Fall, see Murray W. Bundy, "Milton's Prelapsarian Adam," in *Milton: Modern Judgments,* ed. Alan Rudrum (London, 1968), pp. 151–72.

links Eve to some figures associated with ominous change. At one point she appears as a naive Pandora, who learns to use the power of beauty to dominate Adam:

> *The genial Angel to our Sire*
> *Brought her in naked beauty more adorn'd,*
> *More lovely then* Pandora, *whom the Gods*
> *Endowd with all thir gifts, and O too like*
> *In sad event, when to the unwiser Son*
> *Of* Japhet *brought by Hermes, she ensnar'd*
> *Mankind with her faire looks, to be aveng'd*
> *Of him who had stole* Joves *authentic fire.*
> (4. 712–19)

This allusion, and the more glancing one to Circe (9. 522), call sufficient attention to Eve's deceitfulness and its tragic consequences for us to see that her charm can have sinister implications. But to identify Eve as a literary descendant of Tasso's Armida and Spenser's Acrasia, as some critics have, is to seize upon one strand of the web.[2] Other allusions lead in different directions.

The pastoral strain in Eve's literary ancestry is at least as important as her kinship with the seductive women of previous Renaissance epics. When she awes Satan with her simple charms, like a "fair Virgin" of the countryside overcoming someone "long in populous City pent" (9. 445), she more nearly resembles Shakespeare's Perdita or Spenser's Pastorella than Acrasia:

2. I am thinking particularly of the arguments of John M. Steadman and Bartlett Giamatti. See Steadman's *Milton and the Renaissance Hero* (Oxford, 1967), chap. 5, "The Critique of *Amor*," especially p. 120, and Giamatti's *The Earthly Paradise in the Renaissance Epic* (Princeton, 1966), pp. 302–330. Despite a disagreement in emphasis, I am indebted to Steadman's illuminating discussion of the "romantic theme" in *Paradise Lost* with reference to previous epics.

*Her Heav'nly forme*
*Angelic, but more soft, and Feminine,*
*Her graceful Innocence, her every Aire*
*Of gesture or lest action overawd*
*His Malice.*

(9. 457–61)

For a moment it appears that the power of goodness, in the form of Eve's irresistible beauty, has neutralized Satan's evil. In a comparable situation Comus is briefly entranced by the "Divine enchanting ravishment" of the Lady's song. But instead of endowing chaste beauty with supernatural powers, romance fashion, Milton made the outcome depend upon a trial of virtue in each instance.

Eve's radiant femininity is completely unselfconscious, needless to say. In explaining to Raphael Eve's power over him Adam cites "those graceful acts / Those thousand decencies that daily flow / From all her words and actions" (8. 600–602). Perhaps such grace should be described as "Angelic" rather than rustic, but it obviously depends upon the association of innocence with a pastoral mode of life. One cannot explain it, any more than one can explain the grace of Perdita, except by pointing to an instinctive sympathy with nature that seems both the proof and the source of innocence.

Florizel's yearning to freeze Perdita at a particular moment in time reveals a sense of evanescence absent from most of Milton's comments on Eve's grace:

*When you do dance, I wish you*
*A wave o'th'sea, that you might ever do*
*Nothing but that; move still, still so,*
*And own no other function.*

(*The Winter's Tale*, 4. 4. 140–43)

Perdita herself laments the passing of the early spring flowers, in terms which remind us that she inhabits a fallen world:

> *O Proserpina,*
> *For the flowers now that, frighted, thou let'st fall*
> *From Dis's wagon!*
>
> (*W.T.*, 4.4.116–18)

But Perdita is very much like Eve in her feeling for the ways of "great creating nature," especially in her knowledge of flowers and her proprietary interest in them. To Florizel she is "no shepherdess, but Flora / Peering in April's front" (4.4.2–3).

Although Eve does not need a garland for adornment like Perdita or Pastorella, she is loveliest when surrounded by flowers: in the nuptial bower, or half concealed by roses, "Veild in a Cloud of Fragrance" (9. 425), when Satan comes upon her. Whatever their normal season, Eden's flowers bloom continuously in the eternal spring of the Garden, and Eve's beauty seems to share in their freshness. Perdita is also a creature of the spring, and so is another pastoral heroine who anticipates Eve, Earine of Jonson's unfinished pastoral drama, *The Sad Shepherd*:[3]

> *Who had her very being, and her name,*
> *With the first knots or buddings of the Spring,*

3. The verse is too good for Earine's comically melancholy lover Aeglamour, who here laments her apparent drowning. Earine herself seems out of place in Jonson's spirited, greenwood adventure of Robin Hood and his men. Greg notes that her name is the only one not derived from popular romance and that it is a coinage, meaning spirit of the spring. See W. W. Greg, *Pastoral Poetry and Pastoral Drama* (Oxford, 1905), p. 297.

*Borne with the Primrose, and the Violet,*
*Or earliest Roses blowne: when* Cupid *smiled,*
*And* Venus *led the* Graces *out to dance,*
*And all the Flowers, and Sweets in Natures lap,*
*Leap'd out, and made their solemne Conjuration,*
*To last, but while she liv'd.*

1.5. 43–51)

In these lines she seems nymphlike, as Eve often does. We can readily imagine either joining the dance of the Graces.

Eve presides over the flowers in the Garden like a goddess whose touch has the power to inspire growth. Milton pictures her retiring from the presence of Adam and Raphael to walk forth majestically

*Among her Fruits and Flours,*
*To visit how they prosper'd, bud and bloom,*
*Her Nurserie; they at her coming sprung*
*And toucht by her fair tendance gladlier grew.*

(8. 44–47)

Eve's outcry at the prospect of losing her flowers could almost be a lament for lost children, though Milton was not simply making a comment about her maternal instincts:

*O flours,*
*That never will in other Climate grow,*
*My early visitation, and my last*
*At Eev'n, which I bred up with tender hand*
*From the first op'ning bud, and gave ye Names,*
*Who now shall rear ye to the Sun, or ranke*
*Your Tribes, and water from th'ambrosial Fount?*

(11. 273–79)

Eve appears here as patron and guardian of the flowers of Eden, almost a genius of the place. In the fallen world her role is taken over by a figure such as the Genius of the Wood in *Arcades,* who is endowed with the power to save the plants from "noisome winds, and blasting vapours chill." His ministrations must be regarded as secret and magical:

*When Ev'ning gray doth rise, I fetch my round*
*Over the mount, and all this hallow'd ground,*
*And early ere the odorous breath of morn*
*Awakes the slumb'ring leaves, or tassell'd horn*
*Shakes the high thicket, haste I all about,*
*Number my ranks, and visit every sprout*
*With puissant words and murmurs made to bless.*
(54–60)

All readers of *Paradise Lost* know that Adam names the animals, but how many are aware that Eve names the flowers (one of Milton's more interesting additions to the narrative of Genesis)? If we recognize the special sympathy with nature that this act reveals, Milton's comparison of Eve with Flora (Adam awakens Eve "with voice, / Milde, as when *Zephyrus* on *Flora* breathes" [5. 15–16]) seems especially apt. Perdita only plays at Flora to please Florizel—she complains to him that she is a "poor lowly maid, / Most goddess-like prank'd up" (4.4.9–10)—but Milton made Eve a Christian equivalent for Flora, and for Pales, Ceres, and Pomona, the trio of rustic goddesses who have charge of flocks, grain, and fruits respectively. The comparison with Pomona is particularly happy. Entertaining Raphael in her "Silvan Lodge," "that like *Pomona's* Arbour smil'd" (5. 378), Eve assembles her dinner with a sure instinct for what to choose and how to order her fruits: "Taste after taste upheld with kindliest charge" (5. 336).

But Eve most nearly fills the role of Flora, Ovid's *mater*

*florum* (*Fasti* 5. 183). Ovid describes Flora's games as wanton, and in fact Flora came to be regarded in the Renaissance as a goddess of questionable moral character. According to one tradition, cited approvingly by E. K. in his notes to Spenser's March eclogue, Flora was a Roman courtesan who became a goddess.[4] Milton's allusion to Flora has none of these associations, but the myth of Zephyrus and Flora carries with it the suggestion of sensual pleasure. In Ovid's version of the myth Flora was formerly the nymph Chloris ("Chloris eram, quae Flora vocor" [*Fasti,* 5. 195]), whom Zephyrus carried off as his bride and gave the government of flowers. By virtue of the comparison with Zephyrus and Flora, Adam and Eve are identified with the spring landscape and seem to share in the *eros* that animates the natural world.

The most difficult thing to grasp about Milton's Eve is how she can possess both the innocence of a Perdita and the sensuality of Flora, or of Venus, whom she is said to excel in beauty. Milton's insistence on the purity of Eve's love does a great deal to resolve the apparent contradictions in her nature. References to Eve as "our general Mother" and to Adam pressing her "Matron lip / With kisses pure" frame the remarkably sensual description of Adam and Eve embracing ("half her swelling Breast / Naked met his under the flowing Gold / Of her loose tresses hid" [4. 495–97]). She can accept Adam's caresses without losing her modesty, or the grave dignity with which Milton endows her as well as Adam:

4. See Julius S. Held, "Flora, Goddess and Courtesan," in *De Artibus Oposcula XL, Essays in Honor of Erwin Panofsky,* ed. Willard Meiss (New York, 1961), pp. 201–18, for a discussion of Flora's ambiguous character. I am indebted to Kathleen Williams' *Spenser's World of Glass* (Berkeley and Los Angeles, 1966), for the reference.

*Fairest of Creation*

*In thir looks Divine*
*The image of thir glorious Maker shone;*
*Truth, wisdome, Sanctitude severe and pure.*
(4. 291–93)

Confronted by moral asides such as this one, we could never suspect Eve of Flora's wantonness. We might even forget her charm. But even Milton's solemn declaration of the holiness of marriage ("Haile wedded Love") modulates into a description of Cupid's revels: "Here Love his golden shafts imploies, here lights / His constant Lamp, and waves his purple wings" (4. 763–64). We are never far from reminders of the pleasures of love in Eden and the magnetism of Eve's beauty.

When Adam embraces Eve, he smiles,

*With superior Love, as* Jupiter
*On* Juno *smiles, when he impregns the Clouds*
*That shed* May *Flowers.*
(4. 499–501)

In venturing such a comparison Milton could trust the reader to screen out inappropriate thoughts of Olympian quarrels and infidelities, because he had established the idea of Eve's innocence so firmly. The passage suggests the majesty of our "grand parents" and their lordship over nature. Here Juno is indirectly associated with the generative force of nature. It does not matter whether we think of Eve as Flora, or Juno, or Venus (either the Lucretian *Venus genetrix* or the Venus whose birth from the sea Milton described in his fifth Latin elegy) as long as we recognize the spirit of surging life that she embodies.[5] This spirit resembles the *eros* that Milton cele-

5. Frank Kermode suggests that the allusion points to both of these Venuses. See "Adam Unparadised," *The Living Milton,* ed. Kermode (London, 1960), p. 89.

brated in frankly sensual terms in his fifth elegy, on the renewal of Earth's love affair with Phoebus, but it is *eros* sanctified.[6] It can be found in another form in the erotic poetry of the Song of Songs, which Milton echoed in the invitation to arise and go to the fields that Adam breathes like Zephyrus into Eve's ear.

Allusions cluster most thickly about Eve as she takes her leave of Adam, on the point of losing her elusive aura of beauty and grace by the very womanly act of giving in to Satan's urgings. Ironically, Eve ceases to appear goddess-like when she begins to conceive of herself as a goddess under the influence of Satan's seductive flattery. We can imagine her radiance waning as her new self-awareness grows.

*Who sees thee? (and what is one?) who shouldst be seen*
*A Goddess among Gods, ador'd and serv'd*
*By Angels numberless, thy daily Train.*

(9. 546–48)

The Fall demythologizes Eve. Before her act we can think of her as preeminent among women and goddesses in her charm, beauty, and innocent sensuality. Afterward, she appears as a particular, sinful woman.

Milton's comparison of Eve with "*Pomona* when she fled / *Vertumnus*" and with "*Ceres* in her Prime, / Yet Virgin of *Proserpina* from *Jove*" (9. 394–96) anticipates the Fall by hinting at her vulnerability. The allusion to Diana is more poignant because of its ironic overtones:

6. O. B. Hardison discusses the erotic imagery in Milton's account of the Creation and argues that in the larger context of *Paradise Lost* the sexuality of Adam and Eve "is revealed as a special form of the force that is universal in the visible world. This force is the divine *eros*, and to question it is a kind of blasphemy." See *Milton Studies* (Pittsburgh, 1969), 1:160–63.

*Soft she withdrew, and like a Wood-Nymph light,*
Oread *or* Dryad, *or of* Delia's *Train,*
*Betook her to the Groves, but* Delia's *self*
*In gate surpass'd and Goddess-like deport.*
(9. 386–89)

Eve may carry herself like Diana, but she shows a promiscuous readiness to respond to Satan's invitation. Perhaps Milton meant us to recall that Pomona listened to the skillful pleading of Vertumnus, come to argue his case in the guise of an old woman, and then yielded when he threw off his garments to dazzle her with his naked splendor. Hers was not a simple case of rape.

Proserpina, on the other hand, was a wholly innocent victim of infernal power, and when we see Eve surrounded by her roses, herself the "fairest unsupported Flour, / From her best prop so farr, and storm so nigh" (9. 432–33), we feel the same sympathy for her that we do for Proserpina. We know, though, that Eve is "so farr" from help because of her own willfulness and indiscretion. Her situation recalls that of Spenser's Serena, who, having been surprised with her lover by Calidore, in her shame wanders off to pick flowers, only to be seized and carried away by the Blatant Beast.[7] The simile in which Milton introduces the Proserpina myth suggests the frailty of beauty without any hint of blame:

*Not that faire field*
*Of* Enna, *where* Proserpin *gathering flours*
*Herself a fairer Floure by gloomie* Dis
*Was gatherd, which cost* Ceres *all that pain*
*To seek her through the world.*
(4. 268–72)

7. See *The Faerie Queene,* 6.3.20–24. Spenser describes Serena as "loosely wandring" among fields of flowers, "as liking led / Her wavering lust after her wandring sight."

Milton anticipated this peculiarly powerful evocation of doomed innocence in the elegy, "On the Death of a Fair Infant," in which he drew upon the ancient association of flowers with early death.[8] In the more diffuse and improbable mythological conceit of that poem, Winter, imitating the rape of Orithyia by "grim *Aquilo,*" carries off young Anne Philips, the "fairest flower no sooner blown but blasted." Milton's identification of Eve with the flowers of the Garden simultaneously enhances her beauty and reminds the reader of its extreme precariousness. We know that flowers fade, and that Eve is the cause of their fading. Like the rape of Proserpina, her fall ushers in devouring time and the cycle of the seasons, for Satan brings winter as well as death into the Garden.

In Claudian's *De raptu Proserpinae* Jupiter decrees the fate of Proserpina, as God providentially orders Eve's fall in *Paradise Lost,* but Eve chooses her own fate by the exercise of free will, Milton repeatedly reminds us, unlike the totally defenseless Proserpina. She is not swept up by the lord of the underworld in a chariot drawn by black horses, as in Claudian's version of the myth, or carried off by Aquilo, but allows Satan to lead her to the tree and persuade her to eat.

In his initial horror at Eve's sin, Adam calls her "Defac't, deflourd, and now to Death devote" (9. 901). "Deflourd" is one of those serious puns, like "fruitless," that Milton used to good effect in *Paradise Lost.* Eve not only loses her innocence by eating the fruit; she changes roles. We can no longer imagine her as Flora, or Perdita, or even as a rural harvest queen, the closest

8. See Don Cameron Allen, *The Harmonious Vision* (Baltimore, 1953), pp. 47–50, on Milton's use of mythology in the poem and on the fading rose as a symbol in epitaphic verse.

equivalent to Perdita that Milton suggests. The fading of Adam's roses confirms the intrusion of time into the Garden and also the fact of Eve's shame. They fade as if to deny her appearance of chaste beauty.

In their differing ways Jonson's masque *Chloridia* and Fletcher's *The Faithful Shepherdess* depend upon the assumption that forces of disruption or evil can be overcome by the greater power for good inherent in nature. The antimasquers in *Chloridia,* brought up from the underworld by an unruly Cupid, include jealousy, fear, and dissimulation along with such hostile natural forces as rain and the winds. Chloridia ("Queen of the flowers, and Mistris of the Spring") overwhelms them by her presence, with the aid of attendant rivers and fountains and the figure of spring (summoned by Zephyrus to begin the masque). The masque form demands that her victory be total.

In Fletcher's play the shepherdess Clorin works miracles of healing through a special knowledge of herbs made possible by her chastity. The lust of the Sullen Shepherd and of the wanton shepherdesses Cloe and Amarillis is the source of the confusions and injuries on which the plot turns, but so great is Clorin's power that she can heal any wound as long as the victim will banish all unchaste thoughts from his mind. Her efforts, reinforced by those of Pan's priests (guardians of chastity according to Fletcher's curious conception of Pan) and of the God of the River, who heals the wounded virgin Amoret with a flower and a drop of his water, are sufficient to counteract the effects of lust.

Milton's Sabrina, a "Virgin pure" metamorphosed into the goddess of the Severn, combines attributes of both Clorin and the river god. Sabrina's power to release the Lady from Comus's spell with drops from her "fountain pure," though it may suggest the operation of Christian grace in the framework of the poem, seems to spring from the river itself. It is as though Sabrina by virtue of her own purity can call upon a power for goodness latent in the natural world. She is able to extend this power to the surrounding countryside, protecting neighboring herds from fairies and elves:

*For which the Shepherds at their festivals*
*Carol her goodness loud in rustic lays,*
*And throw sweet garland wreaths into her streams.*
(848–50)

One need not suppose that Milton believed in such gifts as Sabrina's, any more than Fletcher believed in the healing arts of Clorin or Jonson in the ability of Chloridia to calm the elements and spread universal joy. But in each instance the pastoral fiction sustains the illusion that evil can be controlled by natural forces.

*Paradise Lost* recalls these confident ventures in the pastoral mode, despite the fact that its pastoralism is of a radically different sort. The story of the Fall does not allow for a Sabrina or a Clorin, but Eve's failure is presented in such a way that it seems to deny the possibility of the offices they perform. In *Paradise Lost* Milton destroyed the illusion of an inviolable pastoral world; Adam's fading roses suggest not only Eve's alienation from nature but the inability of nature to withstand the presence of sin. By comparison with *Paradise Lost* the pastoral fantasies of Jonson and Fletcher, and to a lesser degree Milton's own masque, seem to slight the power of evil. In *L'Allegro,* Milton's most lighthearted attempt at pastoral, nothing even challenges the "secure delight" that displaces all "eating Cares" and makes life a "Sunshine Holyday." Pastoral could serve Milton in *Paradise Lost* as a means for representing the period of true human innocence, but the continuing struggle with evil in the world demanded another mode. The movement of the poem from apparently secure bliss into sin and disorder demonstrates that grace must originate outside the natural world; consolation and redemption can come only from above, through the agency of Christ. The only valid, or stable, pastoral vision is one based upon the union of the redeemed with God in heaven, seen as a reconstituted Arcadia with God enthroned in its center.

In creating his version of Eden Milton drew upon the Arcadia of pastoral tradition, as well as upon the classical dream of a golden age, in order to surpass and thus discount those ideals; neither could have the same poetic currency after *Paradise Lost*. By summoning the nymphs and goddesses that haunt the Arcadian landscape he could show that Eve excelled them; they establish her beauty and grace in the same way that references to Pan and Faunus authenticate the nuptial bower. But with Satan's victory these mythological beings disappear from paradise along with the legions of friendly angels that actually haunt its pleasant places. When the mythological world reappears in the wilderness in *Paradise Regained* ("Nymphs of *Diana's* train, and *Naiades* / With fruits and flowers from *Amalthea's* horn" [2. 355–56]), it is as a sinister illusion created by Satan and spirits of hell.

Milton confirmed Eve's abrupt descent from graceful innocence to guilt by comparing her with Dalilah:

> *So rose the* Danite *strong*
> Herculean Samson *from the Harlot-lap*

*Of* Philistean Dalilah, *and wak'd*
*Shorn of his strength, They destitute and bare*
*Of all thir vertue.*

(9. 1059–63)

The reference plunges us into the fallen world, where lust is commonplace and ugly. And as any reader of *Samson Agonistes* knows, Milton's insult is worse than calling Eve "whore," since it implies that her treachery is directed against God as well as Adam. Both Adam and Eve suffer a drastic loss of dignity by the comparison. In subsequent comparisons with the Indian herdsman and savages seen by Columbus, they dwindle to crude primitives. But Eve's fall from pastoral innocence seems more complete and more shocking than Adam's, because she has been so fully identified with the beauty of paradise. When Adam in his soliloquy bluntly refers to her as "that bad Woman" (10. 837), we are struck by the magnitude of her change.

As a sinner who can suffer the consequences of sin for herself and her descendants, Eve is more humanly interesting than when she embodies the "spirit of love and amorous delight" (8. 427). We can begin to think of her not as a Proserpina threatened by the underworld but as an actual woman with the capacity for moral growth. The process of her regeneration, which begins with her plea for love ("Forsake me not thus Adam"), leads up to another significant comparison, one by which Milton indicates that both Adam and Eve have recovered a measure of their dignity.

*Yet thir port*
*Not of mean suiters, nor important less*
*Seem'd thir Petition, then when th'ancient Pair*
*In Fables old, less ancient yet then these,*

> Deucalion *and chaste* Pyrrha *to restore*
> *The Race of Mankind drownd, before the Shrine*
> *Of* Themis *stood devout.*
>
> (11. 8–14)

This dignity is clearly on a modest, human scale. Deucalion and Pyrrha are simple exemplars of piety, saved from the flood, like Noah, because of their goodness. In his commentary on the *Metamorphoses* George Sandys noted that Deucalion and Noah were celebrated for their justice and religion. His translation reads in part:

> *None was there better, none more just than Hee:*
> *And none more reverenc't the Gods than Shee.*[9]

Milton's ennobling comparison minimizes the guilt of Adam and Eve and suggests their potential for leading a life of faith and virtue. It also deepens the human drama of the event. Like Deucalion and Pyrrha, Adam and Eve face the future with prayers and tears, waiting uncertainly for guidance. And like Ovid's couple they are burdened by a responsibility for the future of the race but draw strength from their mutual love.

Confident that God has heard them with favor, Adam can hail Eve as "Mother of all Mankind" (11. 159), echoing Raphael's earlier greeting:

> *Haile Mother of Mankind, whose fruitful Womb*
> *Shall fill the World more numerous with thy Sons*
> *Than with these various fruits the Trees of God*
> *Have heap'd this Table.*
>
> (5. 388–91)

9. George Sandys, *Ovid's Metamorphoses Englished* (Oxford, 1832), p. 8.

When Eve receives Raphael, surrounded by her fruits and flowers, she appears more like Pomona or Flora than the future mother of the human race. As long as we can identify her with spring and the unchanging beauty of the Garden, she seems to inhabit a mythical world that does not impinge on our own. It is not until her sin breaks the dance of Pan and the Graces that we truly can see her in a historical context.

Before the Fall Eve's view of life is simpler than Perdita's. Afterwards, her capacity for understanding enlarged by the experience of guilt, she can recognize her new role and be grateful for the chance to fulfill it. The self-awareness that fed Eve's ambition to rise above her human station now takes the form of humility:

*But infinite in pardon was my Judge.*
*That I who first brought Death on all, am grac't*
*The sourse of life.*

(11. 167–69)

Consoled by the prospect that through her "the Promis'd Seed shall all restore" (12. 623), Eve can transfer any remaining affection she may have for the Garden to Adam and accompany him willingly ("thou to mee / Art all things under Heav'n, all places thou" [12. 617–18]). We hear no more about her beauty, because it has become less important than the inner strength that fortifies her for a life outside the Garden. In the fallen world flowers adorn the daughters of Cain. Milton does not renounce the pastoral ideal of graceful innocence; rather, he presents its loss as the price of Eve's metamorphosis into a woman whose seed will save mankind. We give up Flora to gain Mary.

# 6

# THE SHAPE OF EVIL

MILTON'S SATAN CONTINUES TO FASCINATE CRITICS largely because he is so complex and protean a character, far more complex, Martin Evans has shown, than the devil of orthodox Christian tradition as he appeared in previous hexaemeral literature.[1] No one approach fully accounts for his function in *Paradise Lost*. He can be seen as a great tragic figure resembling Macbeth in his damnation (the view of Helen Gardner);[2] as an epic hero in a tradition that Milton discredits; as an infernal opposite to the Son in whom the Son's virtues are parodied. Satan's roles are as various as his disguises; he appears as general of the rebel army, emperor of hell, demagogue, adventurer, "artificer of fraud." One can explain Satan's metamorphoses in terms of his cunning and his hatred of God. What bothers many readers of *Paradise Lost*, though, is that Milton treated his character so rudely,

1. See *"Paradise Lost" and the Genesis Tradition* (Oxford, 1968), pp. 223–31. Evans notes that Milton complicated Satan's motivation by making envy the root cause of the rebellion in heaven and a major factor in the temptation.

2. See "Milton's 'Satan' and the Theme of Damnation in Elizabethan Tragedy," *English Studies*, n.s. 1 (1948):46–66.

repeatedly deflating his heroic posturing with irony or moralizing commentary, humiliating the conqueror of man by turning him into a serpent when he attempts to celebrate his triumph.

Milton's Satan is troublesome because of a tension between the demonic and human aspects of his nature. Helen Gardner has said that Milton gave us a "lost Archangel" rather than the "infernal Serpent" his subject demanded, but there is more of the serpent in Satan than we may want to admit.[3] Satan's freedom to make moral choices seems less real than that of Adam and Eve because we see him not only as a tragic figure, racked by despair, but as the "Fiend," the "Evil One" whose only satisfaction is in annihilating the pleasure and goodness he cannot possess ("only in destroying I find ease" [9. 129]). The role of "Adversary" of God subsumes all Satan's other roles and brands his evil as something outside the range of human experience. However human Satan may appear in his misery and pride, he is driven by a compulsion to resist God that goes beyond the unnatural urges of any character in an Elizabethan drama. His anger is closer to the insatiable wrath of the Satan of the Apocalypse, the Dragon who "Came furious down to be reveng'd on men" (4. 4), than to the wrath of Achilles or that of any other literary predecessor.

While Satan resembles Macbeth in the progressive deepening of his commitment to evil and the irreversibility of his course, his damnation is more terrible than Macbeth's because his rebellion condemns him to a hopeless war against God's whole creation. We can define Macbeth's evil in terms of his growing indifference to

3. Helen Gardner, *A Reading of "Paradise Lost"* (Oxford, 1965), p. 66.

human life and the erosion of his capacity for sympathy. By grasping any means of keeping himself in power Macbeth strips himself of the natural, human consolations of age: "honor, love, obedience, troops of friends." But Satan's acceptance of evil ("Evil be thou my Good" [4. 110]) is a totally negative gesture that strikes at the foundations of a universe created and ruled by God. It is difficult to conceive of the kind of power and satisfaction that he craves in human terms at all. On at least one occasion Satan recognizes the futility of his negative way: "which way shall I flie / Infinite wrauth and infinite despaire?" (4. 73–74). Having set himself against God's infinite goodness, Satan discovers that anger and despair lead only to more anger and despair; his perdition is truly "bottomless."

Satan's strivings may seem vainglorious and even comically ineffectual at times, but from one perspective—that of Eden, or man—he appears as a frightening antagonist. When we see the fallen angels deciding against storming the walls of heaven, the power of hell does not seem at all alarming. But when Satan is shown as a conqueror extending his rule over Eden, as Xerxes subdued Greece, and granting Sin and Death the dominion over nature formerly given Adam by God, this power suddenly takes on a new dimension. Arrayed against a pastoral world, it appears irresistible.

Satan is even more frightening when he appears as a predator come to feed on man: a wolf entering God's fold, a cormorant perched on the Tree of Life "devising death," a vulture journeying from the barren north "To gorge the flesh of Lambs or yeanling Kids / On Hills where Flocks are fed" (3. 434–35). These comparisons imply the destruction of the pastoral world by offering glimpses of the "fierce antipathy" among the creatures that follows the Fall. When Satan stalks the Garden in the shape of a lion, then in that of a tiger "who by chance hath spi'd / In some Purlieu two gentle Fawns at play" (4. 403–4), Adam and Eve seem hopelessly vulnerable. Whereas in most literary Arcadias wolves exist as a stock evil to be exorcised, a danger confined to the periphery of a secure world, Satan is a wolf who threatens the very existence of Eden. His invasion of God's fold anticipates the wolvish clergy denounced with such vehemence in *Lycidas,* but Satan is a more dangerous predator than rapacious bishops, for he violates the original communion between God and man and brings death into the world. Obviously, man cannot escape or defeat this foe without supernatural aid.

By showing Satan as a fiend "bent on his prey" Milton invested him with some of the terror that informs medieval conceptions of a bestial devil. Without demonizing the fallen angels in the manner of Andreini,[4] whose Satan has talons and cloven feet and is served by pride in the form of a savage dog, Milton nevertheless preserved enough of Satan's demonic aspect to suggest the immense capacity for destruction of the powers with which man must reckon. Seen as a predator, Satan has at least a distant kinship with those black, hairy devils with claws and beaks who carry off sinners to their damnation. Sin and Death are of course more closely related to the literary and iconographical tradition of monstrous demons. Milton's description of these "Dogs of Hell" ravaging the earth is as close to pure horror as he comes in *Paradise Lost*. The image of Death snuffing the smell of

4. Milton's approach is closer to that of Grotius, who compares Satan with a cruel lion looking for a flock to devour.

"mortal change," like a scavenger drawn by the "scent of living Carcasses design'd / For death" (10. 277–78), fulfills the promise of the earlier comparison of Satan with a vulture in a particularly terrifying way. Both Sin and Death can be seen as preparing a way for the rest of the infernal powers whose potential for destruction Milton suggests early in the poem by comparing the "numberless" bad angels rising from the fiery lake to the locusts that descended upon Egypt and then to barbarian hordes.

Joseph Summers's analysis of the comic aspects of Satan's initial encounter with Sin and Death gets at the way Milton's allegory deflates the pretensions of hell.[5] The burlesque aspects of Satan's relationship with his offspring provide an occasion for the cold laughter at the expense of evil that Milton seemed to enjoy. But as Summers recognizes, we see Sin and Death from the perspective of earth as well as that of heaven (and that of hell, in which they are heroic). If we are to recognize the horror of the Fall, these creatures must have a gothic as well as a comic side. Milton scarcely could have suggested the hideousness of evil without resorting to allegory, since he was unwilling to compromise Satan's dignity by endowing him with the attributes of a medieval demon. By giving Sin and Death an independent existence, Milton was able to establish them as forces outside of nature driven by a demonic compulsion to destroy it.

Sin and Death hover like specters in the background of the action of Book 9. When Milton says that Eve "knew not eating Death," the irony is deepened by our memory of Death's appearance in Book 2 as a dark, nearly shapeless monster, furious enough to attack anything.

5. See Joseph H. Summers, *The Muse's Method* (Cambridge, Mass.), 1962, chap. 2.

The figure of Sin, with her brood of hell hounds, suggests the inevitable self-torment that Eve will suffer from her perversion of nature. In Milton's conception such agony leads to death ("For Death from Sin no power can separate" [10. 251]). Eve cannot begin to conceive of the forces she has released from hell.

Sin and Death also serve as a commentary on Satan's capacity for self-torment and the "eternal Famine" that he suffers in his inner life. As members of the infernal trinity that Milton opposed to the heavenly one, Satan's offspring must be regarded as extensions of his own nature (as Son and Holy Spirit are extensions of the being of the Father). He cannot be understood apart from them, for his rebellion brings them into existence. Their very presence in the poem illustrates the difficulty of approaching Satan simply as a character in a drama.

In their grotesque way Sin and Death mirror Satan's restlessness and his aggressive impulses. Evil is invariably energetic in *Paradise Lost*. This is not the case in *The Faerie Queene*, as C. S. Lewis has observed. Spenser associated evil with lassitude, disease, disgusting appearances, the temptation to relax, and what Lewis calls the "Waste House" (Mammon's Cave, the House of Busyrane).[6] Lewis does not speculate on the causes of these differences except to suggest that they arise from the requirements of dissimilar forms; as an allegorist Spenser was concerned with the continuing state of a particular sin rather than with the moment of sinful choice.

But one must also consider the nature of Milton's choice of an action. *Comus* with its dangerous wood and temptations to ease and sensual delight is decidedly more

6. See *Spenser's Images of Life*, ed. Alistair Fowler (Cambridge, 1967), pp. 64–73.

Spenserian than *Paradise Lost*. The virtuous society in the masque represents order, as it often does in *The Faerie Queene,* whereas in *Paradise Lost* the natural world furnishes man with the pattern of orderly life. With her emotional tautness and her readiness to combat evil the Lady is rather like Guyon in Book 2 of *The Faerie Queene*. The Elder Brother's image of a militant Diana, while it reflects his naive overconfidence in the power of unaided chastity to withstand evil, aptly illustrates her moral posture. In *Paradise Lost* the energetic, tense character is Satan, who must guard against the influence of goodness in the Garden.

Satan is surprisingly like Spenser's Guyon in the earnestness with which he takes up his mission of destruction, though Satan acts out of pride and envy and Guyon from a dedication to the ideal of temperance. In his Odyssean journey Satan resists the appeal of beckoning stars ("Or other Worlds they seem'd, or happy Isles" [3. 567]), just as Guyon sails past the wandering islands with their promise of paradisal delights. And his sinuous approach to Eve recalls the way Guyon and the Palmer creep up on Acrasia, "through many covert glades, and thickets close" (*F.Q.*, 2. 12. 76).[7] Satan's Acrasia is Eve, who "with rapine sweet" bereaves "His fierceness of the

7. In trying to arouse his fallen legions to heroic valor Satan resembles Tasso's Ubaldo, whose role in entering the false paradise to rescue Rinaldo is analogous to Guyon's in the Bower of Bliss. See *Jerusalem Delivered,* trans. Edward Fairfax (New York, 1963), p. 325:

> *All Europe now and Asia be in war;*
> *And all that Christ adore, and fame have won*
> *In battaile strong, in Syria fighting are. . . .*
> *What letharge hath in drowsiness uppend*
> *Thy courage thus? What sloth doth thee infect?*

fierce intent it brought" (9. 441–42). Guyon must resist appeals to the senses and wreck Acrasia's bower with "rigour pittilesse" to win his victory for temperance, while Satan must maintain the purity of his hatred in order to destroy Eve's innocence.

The suggestion that Satan's adventure is modelled at least in part on Guyon's may seem more plausible if one recognizes the way Milton transformed elements of the Bower of Bliss in presenting his own earthly paradise. By insisting upon the joy of the senses in the prelapsarian world, Milton inverted the image of corrupt and debilitating pleasure that Spenser had created. His treatment of life in paradise demonstrates that God intended man to live in a state of sensuous delight and that in such a world energetic action reflects an assertion of the self in defiance of God. Obedience results in quietness and ease. The irony of Satan's situation, heightened by his resemblance to Guyon, is that he has brought himself to a state where he cannot enjoy the delights of Eden as the loyal angels can. He must resist the softening influence of Eve's beauty because he has chosen the uncomfortable role of the destroyer of life and bliss.

Bartlett Giamatti has suggested that Milton presented Eden as a potential Bower of Bliss, with Eve meant to be seen as an incipient Acrasia.[8] Although Eve bears comparison with Renaissance enchantresses and Adam with those Renaissance knights who resigned their manhood in surrendering to pleasure, Milton emphasized the vitality and joy of the Garden and not its potential for evil. We are given no reason to question the "vegetable gold" of the fruit of the Garden or the gold of Eve's dishevelled

8. See A. Bartlett Giamatti, *The Earthly Paradise in the Renaissance Epic* (Princeton, 1966), pp. 302–30.

hair, as Giamatti does, though such uses of "gold" might well be sinister in *The Faerie Queene*. In alluding to Circe (the beasts are "more duteous" at Eve's call "Than at *Circean* call the Herd disguis'd" [9. 522]), Milton hinted at woman's capacity for deceit and man's for lust, but Eve is far from becoming a Circe figure. Although she is the cause of sin in Adam, she does not enslave him. Milton's real concern was with the consequences of sin in both Adam and Eve, especially with the way they come under the tyranny of "sensual Appetite." Lust, in Adam or Eve, is less important than the profound internal disorder from which it arises.

Observing the effect on Satan of his own sin prepares us for the eruption of passion in Adam and Eve. Although Satan regards himself as free, he is, unlike Guyon, incapable of regulating his feelings. He may think that he embraces hatred, but he is in fact possessed by it and by the despair with which it alternates. With its "Floods and Whirlwinds of tempestuous fire" (1. 77) and its allegorized rivers, the landscape of hell reflects the inner turbulence of its inhabitants:

> *Abhorred* Styx *the flood of deadly hate,*
> *Sad* Acheron *of sorrow, black and deep;*
> Cocytus, *nam'd of lamentation loud*
> *Heard on the rueful stream; fierce* Phlegeton
> *Whose waves of torrent fire inflame with rage.*
> (2. 577–81)

These "baleful streams," and the burning lake into which they empty, suggest the violent and self-destructive tendencies of passion.

The soliloquy on Mount Niphates at the beginning of Book 4 provides Milton's most telling illustration of the way Satan's own passions constitute an inner hell. Milton makes a point of the fact that he can no more conceal these passions—they distort his features and reveal his presence to Uriel—than he can escape them. Satan recognizes in the course of his soliloquy that the only way he can escape the tyranny of passion is by subjecting himself to the will of God. At this point, at least, he appears to see that the only real ease is to be found not in destruction but in love. Perhaps he admits to himself the truth of Abdiel's shrewd characterization: "Thyself not free, but to thyself enthrall'd" (6. 181). But by rebelling Satan has opened a Pandora's box of disorderly emotions, and he cannot return to his previous state of calm. One senses that his pride is no longer manageable, if indeed it ever was. Even when Satan seems most like an Elizabethan tragic hero, in this probing soliloquy, we are reminded that his role of Adversary of God is unique and inescapable.

Satan reaffirms his hatred, goes on to win his illusory victory over man, and thereafter must participate in the annual ritual of eating fruit that turns to bitter ashes. Regarded simply as evidence of God's power over Satan, this punishment seems crudely degrading. But it can also be seen as a grotesque demonstration of the power of sin to imbrute and enslave. A hard justice requires that Satan harbor in extreme form the desires that he has aroused in Adam and Eve and then find them frustrated. Such a fate illustrates as well the way Satan is mastered by his passions; it is a symbolic exaggeration of his own bondage to sin.

The experience of Satan reveals some of the forms that the tyranny of passion can assume. His example also demonstrates that passion preys on others, for this is the disturbing implication of all the comparisons of Satan to predators. Satan's rage and envy must find an outlet in aggression, and Adam and Eve are his natural prey. They have no more chance than the "gentle brace, / Goodliest of all the forest" (11. 188–89) that they see pursued by a beast just before Michael's arrival. But Adam and Eve are finally victims of their own passions, and these passions turn them into predators of another sort. The comparisons I have been discussing augur a change from peaceableness to aggression that affects man as well as the beasts. When he eats the fruit, Adam lusts after Eve for the first time. And in the aftermath of their initial excitement Adam and Eve turn on each other with sudden hostility.

Before Satan's arrival in Eden the stability of the emotional life of Adam and Eve is preserved by a subtle inner equilibrium between spiritual and sensual impulses. Milton's explanation of how they lose this equilibrium could not be plainer. When Adam talks about the "commotion strange" of passion that he experiences in Eve's presence, Raphael abruptly warns him against letting passion sway his judgment. God had cautioned him previously: "govern well thy appetite, lest sin / Surprise thee, and her black attendant Death" (7. 546–47). Milton's description of the emotional turbulence that results from the Fall—Adam and Eve are shaken by "high Passions, Anger, Hate, Mistrust, Suspicion, Discord" (9. 1122–23)—demonstrates how completely they have lost control of appetite:

> *Understanding rul'd not, and the Will*
> *Heard not her lore, both in subjection now*
> *To sensual Appetite, who from beneath*
> *Usurping over sovran Reason claim'd*
> *Superior sway.*
>
> (9. 1127–31)

This kind of analysis explains how Adam and Eve have failed, but it gives no indication at all of the bliss they experienced while understanding ruled the passions. Nor does Raphael's sober discussion of love:

> *Love refines*
> *The thoughts, and heart enlarges, hath his seat*
> *In Reason, and is judicious, is the scale*
> *By which to heav'nly Love thou may'st ascend,*
> *Not sunk in carnal pleasure.*
>
> (8. 589–93)

We expect this insistence upon the rational basis of love from Milton. His attention in Book 4 to the joy of the senses is more remarkable.

To explain Milton's success in the difficult task of conveying the bliss of "unlibidinous" love, of pleasure that is not "carnal," one would have to consider his treatment of the Garden as a whole, for the love of Adam and Eve absorbs the vitality and beauty of its setting. Far from being enervating, pleasure has the vibrance and freshness of nature in the prelapsarian world. One can accept this miraculously "vernal" love because Adam and Eve so clearly belong in the Garden. The nuptial bower, a place obviously intended for love, awaits them, and nature provides their epithalamium:

> *Joyous the Birds; fresh Gales and gentle Airs*
> *Whisper'd it to the Woods, and from thir wings*
> *Flung Rose, flung Odors from the spicy Shrub,*
> *Disporting, till the amorous Bird of Night*
> *Sung Spousal, and bid haste the Ev'ning Star*
> *On his Hill top, to light the bridal Lamp.*
>
> (8. 515–20)

The vigorous movement of the verse suggests that nature urges their love and somehow participates in its joyousness. The bower itself, Milton's unusually rich version of a familiar pastoral motif, suggests the delicacy of love in the Garden, and also its sanctity, since this bower is provided by God. By naming Pan and Faunus Milton exorcised their lusts, as if to purify the Arcadian bower for the innocent pleasure of Eden.

Love reigns and revels in the bower of Adam and Eve, Milton tells us, and not in "Court Amours" or in the "bought smile / Of Harlots" (4. 765–66). Both kinds of love that Milton associates with the fallen world are libidinous, one frankly predatory, the other, found in "wanton Mask, or Midnight Ball," a devious battle of the sexes. One would expect to find in court amours the "honor dishonorable" that Milton, following the example of Tasso in the *Aminta,*[9] banished from his Christian Arcadia, and also a competitive spirit alien to pastoral. Although one finds frustrated lovers in pastoral poetry, their frustrations are usually assuaged, and competition tends to be channeled into innocuous forms (singing matches never end in fights). Adam and Eve present a picture of perfect harmony, lulled by nightingales and showered with roses as they sleep embracing, because their love is so purely selfless. Their innocence depends in part upon ignorance of the possibilities for self-satisfaction and self-advancement.

By showing the delicate interdependence of Adam and Eve Milton was able to present a truly unlibidinous love,

9. See Frank Kermode's comments on Tasso's indictment of tyrannical honor in his famous chorus, "O bella étà de l'oro," in "Adam Unparadised," *The Living Milton,* ed. Kermode (London, 1960), pp. 110–11.

wholly free of the kind of desire that arises from a need to use or control someone else. Their love owes its stability to a mutual recognition of Adam's superiority, but subjection is natural and easy for Eve because "requir'd with gentle sway" (4. 308). She yields willingly, with "coy submission, modest pride, / And sweet, reluctant, amorous delay" (4. 310–11). This submissiveness cannot be confused with the subjection of woman to man that the Son decrees after the Fall ("hee over thee shall rule" [10. 196]). It is harder to distinguish between Adam's natural susceptibility to Eve's charms, which ensures the equilibrium of their relationship, and a yielding to passion that threatens this equilibrium. At what point does innocent desire become a passion that undermines the sovereignty of reason? We can only judge by the one critical instance, when devotion to Eve blurs Adam's sense of prior duty to God to the point where he can eat the fruit she offers.

The concupiscence of Adam and Eve after the Fall had the same kind of importance for Milton that it did for Augustine.[10] Their love is one manifestation of a general indulgence of appetite that results from relaxing the control of reason. In *Christian Doctrine* Milton defined original sin as the "evil concupiscence" of which Adam and Eve were first guilty and which they transmitted to their descendants in the form of an "innate propensity" to sin.[11] This concupiscence includes the gluttony to which Eve abandons herself in eating the fruit ("Greedily she ingorg'd without restraint" [9. 791]), as well as

10. See the excellent discussion by Evans, *"Paradise Lost" and the Genesis Tradition* (Oxford, 1968), pp. 98–99, of Augustine's doctrine of concupiscence and its influence.

11. CE, 15:193.

Adam's lust; uncontrolled desire wells up in a similar way in each case, and both passions embody the rage for self-satisfaction that is the sign of *cupiditas*.

Adam's lust, reciprocated by Eve, differs from his innocent love in its excessiveness and in the sense in which it treats Eve as an object. It is greedy, as lust is for Spenser, though it does not assume the subhuman forms that lust does in *The Faerie Queene* (for example, the "greedie Lust" of the savage man who pursues Amoret in Book 4 or the furious beasts outside the Bower of Bliss). Shakespeare compares the lecherous Tarquin with a falcon in *The Rape of Lucrece* and gives Venus the appetite of a hawk in *Venus and Adonis*.[12] Donne, in "Love's Diet," speaks playfully of his "buzard love." What we see in Adam after he eats the fruit is a more sinister "buzard love," hot and fierce where his former affection for Eve was tender.

Adam's "lascivious Eyes" recall the "greedily depasturing delight" with which Acrasia looks at Verdant, consuming her victim with her desire as mechanically as sheep strip a meadow. The lingering gaze is usually a danger signal in *Paradise Lost*. We first encounter it in Eve's dream: in Satan's suspicious praise of the magnetism of Eve's charms ("In whose sight all things joy, with ravishment / Attracted by thy beauty still to gaze" [5. 46–47]) and in Eve's description of Satan gazing at the tree. Eve should recognize that if all living things do indeed "gaze on" her and adore her "Celestial Beauty," as Satan claims in the actual temptation, such worship is misplaced. But she is too pleased with Satan's flattery to be critical. Meanwhile, the fruit solicits her "longing eye"

12. Tarquin is also compared to a lion, a wolf, and a buzzard.

and she responds: "Fixt on the Fruit she gaz'd" (9. 735). By allowing herself to gaze, Eve already has taken the first step toward sin.[13] In yielding she gives in to the urgings of her senses as well as to the pride aroused by Satan's arguments. Her obliviousness to everything but the fruit, "Intent now wholly on her taste" (9. 786), is proof of how completely she has lost control over her responses.

When Adam looks at Eve with lascivious eyes, he is already trapped by the tyranny of the affections.[14] Michael's explanation in Book 12 of the reason for man's subjection to the rule of tyrants suggests what it is to be a "servant of sin" (John 7:34):

> *Reason in man obscur'd, or not obey'd,*
> *Immediately inordinate desires*
> *And upstart Passions catch the Government*
> *From Reason, and to servitude reduce*
> *Man till then free.*
>
> (12. 86–90)

The sea of irascible passions that engulfs Adam and Eve

13. William Madsen cites Donne's comment, "The eye is the devils doore," in the course of extended discussion of the superiority of the ear over the eye as an organ of understanding for Protestant thinkers. He begins by discussing the deceptiveness of Eve's "fair" appearance. See *From Shadowy Types to Truth* (New Haven, 1968), especially p. 162.

14. Compare Milton's description of the sons of Seth in the tents of wickedness:

> *The Men, though grave, ey'd them, and let thir eyes*
> *Rove without rein, till in the amorous Net*
> *Fast caught, they lik'd, and each his liking chose.*
>
> (11. 585–87)

Spenser's Cymochles is more furtive, stealing glimpses of Acrasia while pretending to sleep: "And his frayle eye with spoyle of beauty feedes."

when they awake seems to be released by the concupiscible passions to which they yielded earlier. Concupiscence is only the beginning, as Adam recognizes when he begins to understand the implications of their actions: "in our Faces evident the Signs / Of foul concupiscence: *whence evil store*" (9. 1078–79). The "fierce passion"(10. 865) that succeeds Adam's first rush of shame recalls Satan's emotional state ("fierce" is Milton's favorite adjective for describing Satan's desires).

If the Fall were to turn Eden into a Bower of Bliss, we might expect Adam and Eve to be reduced to immobility by their lust, or Adam to languish in the power of Eve like a disabled Mars, but in *Paradise Lost* sin enslaves by producing inner torment. To embrace evil is to enter a state of continual agitation, the antithesis of the peace to be found in obedience to God. *The Faerie Queene* is littered with the victims of pride, lust, despair, and the other sins, who are often found in some kind of prison;[15] spiritual torpor is the most frequent result of sin for Spenser. Milton's protagonists, Satan as well as Adam and Eve, are not imprisoned by sin but racked by the agonies produced by "upstart Passions" and an uneasy conscience. The drama of Adam and Eve after the Fall is largely the story of how they suffer from and eventually come to control the "perturbations" that arise from their sin.

When the Son intercedes for the repentant Adam and Eve with the Father, he describes their prayers as the first fruits of "thy implanted Grace in Man" (11. 23). In *The Faerie Queene* the intervention of grace is likely to be sudden and decisive, as in the appearance of Arthur

15. They may, of course, be possessed by fury, like Pyrochles in Book 2.

with his diamond shield to rescue Redcross from Orgoglio's castle, but "Prevenient grace" works invisibly in Adam and Eve.[16] To explain these differing treatments of the action of grace by saying that Spenser conceived of it allegorically and Milton dramatically, or that grace is externalized in *The Faerie Queene* and internalized in *Paradise Lost,* would not do justice to Milton's extreme concern with individual moral action. Adam's spiritual *agon* is closer to the struggle with sin that Bunyan recounts in *Grace Abounding* than to anything in *The Faerie Queene*. One must recognize the intensity of his inner drama and the way it turns on the decision to forgive Eve. The invisible effects of grace may prompt Eve to ask forgiveness and Adam to respond to her show of love (removing "the stony from thir hearts" [11. 4]), but these appear as individual acts of will. Thus Adam and Eve prove themselves capable of finding their way back to God, as Satan could not. They take the first steps toward freeing themselves from sin and its perturbation.

Love can give Adam and Eve a measure of peace because it frees them from their obsessive self-concern. Adam despairs of finding a way out of the "Abyss of fears / And horrors" (9. 843–44) into which his conscience has driven him, but once he has felt "Commiseration" for Eve in her contrition a way presents itself. In granting her the "peace" she asks he discovers that they may relieve each other's woe by striving "In offices of Love."[17] From the "contempt of life and pleasure" (10. 1013) that leads Eve to propose suicide we know that

16. See the discussion of Milton's conception of grace by C. A. Patrides, *Milton and the Christian Tradition* (Oxford, 1966), pp. 203–14.

17. See 10. 912–13, 938.

her recovery from the incapacitating effects of sin is far from complete at this point. It is not until they humble themselves completely, before God, that she or Adam feels a resurgence of hope.

Even after he has repented, man must be educated in the workings of sin if he is to learn to manage his affections. Michael's grisly tableau of the diseased is intended to teach Adam the lesson of temperance, "The rule of not too much" (11. 531). All the agonies of the lazar house, in Michael's providential view of the origins of disease, can be regarded as punishment for serving "ungovern'd appetite." Each of the various tableaux of Book 11 illustrates some failure of reason to govern the passions: Cain's murder of Abel, the lust of the sons of Seth, the violence of the giants, and the riot and luxury that grow out of conquest.

Michael teaches Adam how the individual man may learn to recognize and avoid sin by regulating his appetites. But Sin herself remains a character in the larger cosmic drama of *Paradise Lost* and must be dealt with in the terms of that drama, along with Death. Milton's description of Sin and Death about to invade the earth creates the impression that man has no defenses against the demonic appetite of these "Furies" of hell, especially "all conquering *Death*." Yet Milton abruptly dispels the horror of the scene by introducing the voice of God, speaking from "his transcendent Seat," thus superimposing the divine perspective on the human. Sin and Death are reduced from scourges of the earth to God's "Hell-hounds" licking up the draff of "man's polluting Sin"; the Son will hurl them through Chaos to "obstruct the mouth of Hell / For ever, and seal up his ravenous Jaws" (10. 636–37).

A gaping hell mouth, usually the gargantuan mouth of Leviathan or some more familiar beast, was one of the commonest features in medieval and Renaissance pictorial renderings of hell.[18] It suggests the distorting effects of sin—one is reduced to a giant mouth by appetites become monstrous—and the punishment that awaits the sinner. Satan himself was often represented with the legs of unfortunate sinners protruding from his mouth.[19] God's promise to seal the "ravenous Jaws" of hell takes on more force if we have such images in mind, as many of Milton's contemporaries would have had. It provides graphic reassurance that Death's "rapacious claim" will be superseded by a higher claim.

Milton gave Death a larger role than Satan in the apocalyptic drama anticipated by the prophecies of Father and Son, exploiting the dramatic implications of the characterization of Death in the first epistle to the Corinthians as "the last enemy that shall be destroyed" (1 Cor. 15:26). Death, not Satan, is the antagonist that the Son declares he will defeat:

*On me let Death wreck all his rage;*
*Under his gloomie power I shall not long*
*Lie vanquisht. . . .*

18. See Robert Hughes, *Heaven and Hell in Western Art* (New York, 1968), pp. 175–88.

19. Milton's Death also resembles the dragon of Book 1 of *The Faerie Queene* in striking ways. Spenser's monster, described as "the damnéd feend" and "hell-bred beast," seems to embody a demonic rage against life:

*his deepe devouring jawes*
*Wide gapéd, like the griesly mouth of hell,*
*Through which into his darke abisse all ravin fell.*
(1.11.12)

He dared not approach the tree of life, Spenser says, "for he was deadly made, / And all that life preservéd, did detest."

*But I shall rise Victorious, and subdue*
*My vanquisher, spoild of his vanted spoile;*
*Death his deaths wound shall then receive, and stoop*
*In glorious, of his mortall sting disarm'd.*
*I through the ample Air in Triumph high*
*Shall lead Hell Captive maugre Hell, and show*
*The powers of darkness bound. Thou at the sight*
*Pleas'd, out of Heaven shalt look down and smile,*
*While by thee rais'd I ruin all my Foes,*
*Death last, and with his Carcass glut the Grave.*
(3. 241–43, 250–59)

The rage too great for man to satisfy is spent on Christ. Death is Milton's equivalent for the devouring time of Shakespeare's sonnets, which appears only as a hollow personification; whatever "The Scythe of Time mows down," Death will "devour unspar'd" (10. 607). In his early poem "On Time" Milton had shown Time glutting himself on all the "mortal dross" of the world and then consuming his own "greedy self." But he transferred these functions to Death in *Paradise Lost,* in the process creating a much more ghastly figure. With the powerful image of Death glutting the grave, a variation on the sealing of hell mouth, Milton effectively degraded this monster and affirmed Christ's invincible might. Such affirmations support the theological scaffolding of *Paradise Lost.* The reader, whose fear of the "Fiend" and his followers Sin and Death Milton plays on so effectively, must be convinced that the "powers of darkness" will prove impotent at last and that death is indeed the "Gate of Life" (12. 571).

Michael's account of how Christ will surprise "The Serpent, Prince of air, and drag in Chains / Through all his Realm, and there confounded leave" (12. 454–55) shows Satan the archangel reduced to Satan the serpent of Revelation bound by Christ. But Milton gave relatively little attention to Satan's ultimate defeat, perhaps out of a reluctance to identify his character too closely with the serpent. Certainly his stature is too great for him to undergo the kind of humiliation that the less imposing Satan of *Paradise Regained* suffers:

*Hereafter learn with awe*
*To dread the Son of God: he all unarm'd*
*Shall chase thee with the terror of his voice*
*From thy Demoniac holds, possession foul,*
*Thee and thy Legions, yelling they shall flye,*
*And beg to hide them in a herd of Swine,*
*Lest he command them down into the deep*
*Bound, and to torment sent before thir time.*
(4. 625–32)

Satan and his "Imperial Powers" are reduced here to demons who can possess individual men (in the most extreme form of the tyranny of sin) but must themselves live under a deferred sentence of bondage and eternal torment.

*Paradise Regained* is built around a paradox that is largely implicit in *Paradise Lost:* the power of the weak to defeat the strong. The scene in which Christ patiently endures all the "terror" that Satan can summon beautifully illustrates the impotence of evil in the presence of faith:

*Infernal Ghosts, and Hellish Furies, round*
*Environ'd thee, some howl'd, some yell'd, some shriek'd,*
*Some bent at thee thir fiery darts, while thou*
*Sat'st unappall'd in calm and sinless peace.*
(4. 422–25)

In the terms of *Paradise Lost* one might say that the lamb defeats the wolf. But the Satan of *Paradise Regained* retains little of the power to terrify and destroy of the Satan of *Paradise Lost.* The key to Satan's stature in *Paradise Lost* is his power: to battle the armies of God for three days in heaven, to subvert the new world of man, and to give Sin and Death possession of this world. The complexity of Satan's motivation and his capacity for doubt as well as defiance make him a protagonist who invites comparison with a Macbeth or a Faustus. But in making such comparisons one must remember that Milton humanized Satan only to a point. In the end, hellish hate and hellish power must be measured on a different scale from human ambition. In Milton's view Satan's will to destroy results from a capacity for evil that exceeds anything in human nature, as the love of the Son for man excels any merely human love.

# 7
# THE IMAGE OF THE CITY

The city serves as a comprehensive symbol of evil in Milton's late works. Gaza, the setting for *Samson Agonistes,* epitomizes the idolatry of the Philistines and their tyranny over the Israelites; when Samson pulls down the columns of the temple of Dagon, he destroys the nobility not only of that city but of "each Philistian city round" (1655), all of them "Drunk with Idolatry, drunk with Wine" (1670). In *Paradise Regained* the great cities of the ancient world, Athens and Jerusalem excepted, represent the power, luxury, and glory that Jesus must reject. For the archetypal city we must look to *Paradise Lost.* We first see Pandaemonium as a temple, suggesting by its splendor the magnitude of hellish idolatry and devotion to luxury, then as a palace and council chamber, and finally as a city:

> *The rest were all*
> *Farr to the inland retir'd, about the walls*
> *Of* Pandaemonium, *Citie and proud seate*
> *Of* Lucifer . . .
>
> . . . *the late*
> *Heav'n-banisht Host, left desert utmost Hell*

*Many a dark League, reduc't in careful Watch*
*Round thir Metropolis.*

(10. 422–25, 436–39)

Milton's comparison of Pandaemonium with Babylon and Cairo suggests that it is to be regarded as the model for these and other centers of empire. Their kings are conquerors and tyrants in the tradition of Satan, and the cities themselves, like Pandaemonium, represent a perversion of the ideal community of heaven.

John M. Steadman has shown that Milton exploited the traditional antithesis between Babylon and Jerusalem in building his epic around the conflict between the kingdoms of earth and heaven instead of national rivalries.[1] He and others have invoked Augustine's concept of the *civitas terrena* and the *civitas Dei* to explain Milton's sense of the warfare between God and Satan in the world:[2]

> Accordingly, two cities have been formed by two loves: the earthly by the love of self, even to the contempt of God; the heavenly by the love of God, even to the contempt of self. The former, in a word, glories in itself, the latter in the Lord.[3]

Augustine thought of these two cities as being represented by Babylon and Jerusalem. For example, in his commen-

1. *Milton and the Renaissance Hero* (Oxford, 1968), pp. 90–93.

2. See Louis Martz, *The Paradise Within* (New Haven, 1964), p. 116; C. A. Patrides, *Milton and the Christian Tradition* (Oxford, 1968), pp. 130–31, 160.

3. *The City of God*, 14.28. From the translation by Marcus Dods (New York, 1950), p. 477.

tary on Psalm 87, he symbolically opposes historic Babylon and Jerusalem:

> By Babylon is meant the city of this world: as there is one holy city, Jerusalem; one unholy, Babylon: all the unholy belong to Babylon, even as all the holy to Jerusalem.[4]

In *Paradise Lost* Milton identifies all cities but Jerusalem with Babylon. Babylon is the city of the world. The historical Jerusalem gets relatively little attention in *Paradise Lost*, and heaven is never referred to as the New Jerusalem, though we see its walls and towers.[5] In *Paradise Regained,* where Jerusalem plays a decisive role in the plot, Milton never pictures heaven as a city. This lack of attention to the city of God is not surprising in view of Milton's preoccupation with the loss and subsequent recovery of paradise and his tendency to make the city an image of human corruption and estrangement from God. In *Paradise Lost* the rise of Babylon is as significant an indication of Satan's conquest of the earth as the destruction of Eden in the flood. City and paradise cannot coexist on earth, because for Milton they were symbols for antithetical states of being.

For Milton and his contemporaries the opposition of the garden and the city, which assumes many forms in pastoral literature and the poetry of retirement, could

4. *Saint Augustin: Expositions on the Book of Psalms,* from *The Nicene and Post-Nicene Fathers,* 1st ser., vol. 8 (New York, 1894). Edited by A. Cleveland Coxe from the Oxford translation.

5. Steadman suggests that Milton preferred to think of heaven as a "kingdom" rather than a city, although he does refer to "our eternall City in Heaven," in *Of Reformation.* See *Milton and the Renaissance Hero,* p. 89 n.

easily take on theological implications. As commentators on Genesis were quick to note, the first city was founded by Cain. Abraham Cowley could assert, in his poem "The Garden": "God the first Garden made, and the first City, *Cain.*" Augustine, who was more interested in the condition of man than in gardening, is perhaps more relevant to Milton: "It is recorded of Cain that he built a city, but Abel, being a sojourner, built none."[6] He characteristically goes on to state that the city of the saints is above. The image of paradise was ultimately more important to Milton than that of the city, but he would have agreed that man became a sojourner on the earth as a result of the Fall. To trust in cities is to forget that we are all, in the words of Hebrews (11:13), "strangers and pilgrims on the earth."

The great image of Babylon in Revelation no doubt colored Milton's view of the world's cities. In its prophesied destruction he saw God's judgment on the "Babylonish merchants of souls" in the Roman church.[7] Yet all the "cities of the nations" are included in the vision of destruction in Revelation (16:19). Babylon signified more than contemporary Rome for Protestants, however freely they might use the term to refer to the church. As Thomas Brightman, writing in the early seventeenth century, would have it, "every powerful, proud, Idolatrous, bloody and wicked Citty, may be called Babylon."[8] Such inclusiveness suggests the famous description of Vanity Fair, which Bunyan expanded to take in all western Europe and practically all the forms of viciousness he could think

6. *The City of God,* 15.1, p. 479.
7. CE, 3, pt. 1:56.
8. *A Revelation of the Revelation* (Amsterdam, 1615), p. 561.

of, from false swearing to murder and adultery. Vanity Fair *is* human society in *The Pilgrim's Progress*. To get to the Celestial City without passing through it one would have to "go out of the World."[9] Milton's treatment of cities in *Paradise Lost* and *Paradise Regained* is more historically oriented and not so bluntly moralistic as Bunyan's, but almost as sweeping. In the apocalyptic perspective of his epics, all cities belong to the City of Destruction.

Milton sounds most Puritan in his condemnation of the sensual indulgence of city life, in *Paradise Lost* associated with Belial:

> *In Courts and Palaces he also Reigns*
> *And in luxurious Cities, where the noyse*
> *Of riot ascends above their loftiest Towrs,*
> *And injury and outrage.*
>
> (1. 497–500)

We can imagine the "insolence" of the sons of Belial producing further injury and outrage in the streets of Sodom. Sensualism does not have the same overtones of violence in *Paradise Regained*, but it is clearly to be found in cities. The "pompous Delicacies" of the banquet with which Satan tempts Jesus seem oddly out of place in the wilderness; Satan himself appears at this point in his campaign as "one in City, or Court, or Palace bred" (2. 300).

The false glory of cities concerned Milton more than their devotion to luxury, however. The monuments "Of Babel / And the works of *Memphian* Kings" (1. 694),

9. *The Pilgrim's Progress*, ed. James Wharey (Oxford, 1960), p. 89.

easily outdone by the builders of Pandaemonium, are bids for glory, as are all displays of wealth and pomp. Such efforts increase in perversity when they involve idolatry, as in the contest of Babylon and Cairo to enshrine their gods with splendor, or in defiance of God, as in Nimrod's attempt to build "A Citie and Towre, whose top may reach to Heav'n" (12. 44). The best criticism of the pursuit of glory is Jesus's answer to Satan in *Paradise Regained:*

*For what is glory but the blaze of fame,*
*The peoples praise, if always praise unmixt?*
*And what the people but a herd confus'd,*
*A miscellaneous rabble, who extol*
*Things vulgar, and well weigh'd, scarce worth the praise.*
(3. 47–51)

True glory is measured by the approbation of God, not the external signs that influence the rabble. Jesus's argument that the most illusory and dangerous kind of glory is that gained by conquerors, who enslave peaceful nations and leave behind "Nothing but ruin whereso'er they rove / And all the flourishing works of peace destroy" (3. 79–80), points to the primary role of cities in Milton's epics; they are objects of siege or places from which war is waged. As seats of empire, cities symbolize the desire for mastery over people and things, the pursuit of power and the pursuit of wealth. Conquerors feed on the spoils of war and the extension of trade that conquest makes possible.

In *The Tenure of Kings and Magistrates* Milton discusses the rise of cities and states from the standpoint of a political theorist, but in *Paradise Lost* cities appear in much the same light as they do in classical accounts of the four ages of civilization—as evidence of the deterioration of life after the Golden Age. In these mythic renderings of history the rise of walled cities testifies to a new atmosphere of mutual hostility.[10] A nascent mercantile spirit, shown in the cutting of pine trees for use in building ships in which to pursue trade, is another sign of the falling off from the Golden Age. Virgil's Evander, recounting the history of Italy for Aeneas, regards greed and the fury of war as inseparable: "belli rabies et amor successit habendi" (8. 327).[11]

In Books 11 and 12 of *Paradise Lost* Milton emphatically associates the destructiveness and hatred of war with the rise of cities:

> *Cities of Men with lofty Gates and Towrs,*
> *Concours in Arms, fierce Faces threatning Warr,*
> *Giants of mightie Bone, and bould emprise.*
> (11. 640–42)

These are the men who lay siege to cities and attack shepherds, inaugurating a period of violence, oppression, and "Sword-Law" that makes impossible any kind of civil order. The scenes in which Milton portrays this violence

10. For example, in the *Metamorphoses,* as translated by Arthur Golding in *Shakespeare's Ovid* (London, 1961), p. 23:

*Men knew no other countries yet, than were* [sic] *themselves did keepe:*
*There was no towne enclosed yet, with walles and ditches deepe.*
*No horne nor trumpet was in use, no sword nor helmet worne.*

In the *Amores* (3.7) Ovid asks why men must take up arms and fortify cities ("turritis incingere moenibus urbes").

11. In Virgil's fourth eclogue, a lingering hostility prompts men to wall their cities and to go to sea in ships, even when Augustus has restored the Golden Age.

are indebted to Homer's description of the shield of Achilles, but Homer's broader vision includes two cities, one associated with weddings and feasting, the other with war.[12] Homer accepts war as a natural human occupation, balancing it with such peaceful activities as harvesting. But Milton uncompromisingly condemns war in the spirit of the sixth chapter of Genesis; mankind must be destroyed because the earth is "full of violence." Milton's giants, progeny of the daughters of Cain, multiply Cain's sin "Ten thousandfold." To the world they are heroes and "great Conquerors, / Patrons of Mankind, Gods, and Sons of Gods," to Milton "Destroyers rightlier call'd and Plagues of men" (11. 695–97).

The few peaceful scenes in the last two books reflect a feeling for biblical pastoral that Milton shared with Du Bartas, who identifies the patriarchs with the goodness of country life:

> Noah *the just, meek* Moses, Abraham
> *(Who* Father of the Faithful Race *became)*
> *Where* [sic] *Shepheards all, or Husbandmen (at least)*
> *And in the Fields passéd their Dayes the best.*[13]

Milton makes the families and tribes that flourish in the peaceful interlude after the flood exemplars of an ideal pastoral community, piously content to live under patriarchal rule "With fair equalitie, fraternal state" (12. 26). In violating this concord, by arrogating "Dominion undeserved / Over his brethren," Nimrod becomes the first tyrant and emperor. Although Nimrod is not linked with

12. *Iliad,* 18, 11. 468–608.
13. *The Complete Works of Joshua Sylvester,* ed. A. B. Grosart (Edinburgh, 1880), 1:49.

Babel in Genesis, it seems inevitable that Milton should have made him a builder of cities.[14] In his account Babel symbolizes a determination to defy God and the tyrannical will to dominate others. It is a primitive Pandaemonium and the earliest version of "that proud City" that establishes its dominion over Jerusalem.

The city in *Paradise Regained* even more clearly signifies conquest—not only Babylon but Nineveh, Persepolis, and all the rest that Satan shows Christ in the course of offering him Parthian power. Rome, the "Imperial City," with its "glittering Spires" and intricate work of "fam'd Artificers," includes all the vices of the city in spectacular form. Milton imaginatively enlarges Roman splendor in order to have Jesus reject it as "grandeur and majestic show / Of luxury" (4. 110–11). In *The History of Britain* Milton saw the collapse of civilization in the fall of Rome before barbarian invaders ("Learning, Valour, Eloquence, History, Civility, even Language"),[15] but in *Paradise Regained* he chose to show the decadence of the empire and the failure of Roman justice. Satan's catalogue of exotic places that mark the geographical limits of Roman rule should be read as a register of exploited peoples. As Jesus says in refusing the power Satan offers, the Romans were once just and mild but now,

*Govern ill the Nations under yoke,*
*Peeling thir Provinces, exhausted all*
*By lust and rapine.*

(4. 135–37)

14. Nimrod was widely regarded by commentators on Genesis as the builder of Babel. See Arnold Williams, *The Common Expositor* (Chapel Hill, 1948), p. 161.
15. CE, 10:101.

In their geographical range, the catalogues of cities in *Paradise Lost* and *Paradise Regained* dramatize the fact that earthly power exists to acquire territory. We measure this power on a map, as we gauge the magnificence of cities by the splendor and size of their walls and buildings. The very breadth of the catalogues reminds us that Adam and Jesus are isolated from human society, one in the Garden and the other in the wilderness, and that their meditations depend upon this isolation. For the cities that Milton enumerates mirror a world of multiplicity and flux from which both Adam and Jesus must learn to detach themselves, in spirit if not in fact, if they are to preserve their respective visions of divine truth. Adam, taught by Michael to recognize God's providence, can take refuge from the labyrinthine particularity of the external world in a "paradise within." The phrase suggests a transference of the simplicity and quiet found in the actual pastoral world of Eden to the inner life.

Milton presents the one good city in *Paradise Regained*, Jerusalem, in such a way that it seems to excel Rome:

> *'Till underneath them fair* Jerusalem,
> *The holy City lifted high her Towers.*
> *And higher yet the glorious Temple rear'd*
> *Her pile, far off appearing like a Mount*
> *Of Alabaster, top't with golden Spires.*
> (4. 544–48)

By one of those shifts in perspective at which Milton is so adept we see Jerusalem as with the eyes of Jesus. It would not appear this way to Satan, or to anyone who calculates beauty, power, and glory by his standards. Jesus's own description of his kingdom is metaphoric:

> *Know therefore when my season comes to sit*

> *On* David's *Throne, it shall be like a tree*
> *Spreading and overshadowing all the Earth*
> *Or as a stone that shall to pieces dash*
> *All Monarchies besides throughout the world,*
> *And of my Kingdom there shall be no end.*
> (4. 146–51)

To think, like Satan, of this kingdom as harboring cities is to reckon divine power in human terms.

In repudiating Rome Milton broke sharply with the epic tradition of celebrating national achievements and the founding of empires.[16] The glorification of Rome in previous epics reveals a profound confidence in the possibilities for secular order and justice. Virgil's Jove promises Venus that he has not set bounds or temporal limits to Roman rule: "imperium sine fine dedi."[17] In the *Aeneid* the founding of a city is a noble occupation and an occasion for joy, as Aeneas's excitement at observing the building of Carthage demonstrates, because it hastens the spread of civilization and social order. Ilioneus describes the city as giving Dido the opportunity to rein proud peoles with justice (1. 523). Dante clung to the idea of the Holy Roman Empire as a means of extending justice and

16. Steadman quotes Tasso's prescription for the matter of epic poetry and goes on to illustrate Milton's rejection of secular monarchy. See *Milton and the Renaissance Hero*, pp. 89–90.

17. *Aeneid*, 1. 278–79. Charles T. Davis quotes Augustine's sharp response to Virgil's claim. See *Dante and the Idea of Rome* (London, 1957), pp. 54–55. Although he could hold up the spirit of the Romans as a model for Christians, Augustine attacked the empire for its preoccupation with temporal power. Christian Rome, on the other hand, could serve God's purposes. See Samuel Kliger, "The 'Urbs Aeterna' in *Paradise Regained*," *PMLA* 71 (1946):479–91, on classical praise of Rome and Milton's rejection of both *urbs aeterna* and *urbs sacra*.

preserving peace. In its pagan as well as its Christian era, Rome was for him an instrument of divine providence. He thought of it as the capital of the Christian empire and the Christian church, and as the city God chose to unify the world.[18] The fact that Dante could use the imperial eagle in the *Paradiso* as a symbol of both Roman and divine justice is revealing.[19] However imperfect human justice may be, it remains an ideal that he could sustain through the example of just rulers and the belief that the justice men achieve is inspired by God.[20]

Milton's rejection of the ideal of human justice as embodied in Rome, given new life in the Renaissance epic by Vida,[21] is in the fullest sense a rejection of the possibility of lasting justice and order on earth before the second coming of Christ. Both Miltonic epics call attention to the discontinuity between human and divine justice. The theme of retribution looms very large in the last two books of *Paradise Lost.* Adam recognizes that disease is a punishment for sin ("I yield it just" [11. 526]), and that death is necessary to satisfy "high Justice" (12. 401). Adam can more readily accept God's vengeance on tyrants (Nimrod and Pharaoh) than on the victims of conquest or oppression, but he must understand that such victims deserve their fate. As Michael explains, when man allows the passions to rule his reason, thus losing his inward liberty, "God in Judgement just / Subjects him from

18. Davis comments at length on the various aspects of Dante's conception of Rome.

19. See especially cantos 18–20.

20. See *Paradiso*, 18, 115–17.

21. Vida's extravagant praise of Rome (see *Christiad*, trans. J. Cranwell [Cambridge, Eng., 1768], 1, 921–30) reflects his hopes for the spread of Christianity and the emergence of a Christian world order under the dominance of Rome.

without to violent Lords" (12. 92–93). Babylon's conquest of Jerusalem is such a divine judgment. The *History of Britain* offers a cyclical pattern of human failure invariably punished by God with disaster.

In *Paradise Lost* Milton repeatedly reminds the reader of the inadequacy, or the complete absence, of human justice. Where Dante's ideal is the just ruler, Augustus or Justinian, Milton's is the one just man in a dark age. Both Enoch and Noah exemplify the "Righteousness" that Milton saw as necessary to justice and peace, and both are rejected by the societies they attempt to reform. The council of elders and military leaders that turns on Enoch so savagely is an appalling example of the failure of reason. Although the Israelites provide a more encouraging model of an earthly community, they are unable to continue living righteously in obedience to God's laws, and their failure demonstrates to Adam the need for Christ to pay for men's sins with his blood:

> *Just for unjust, that in such righteousness*
> *To them by Faith imputed, they may finde*
> *Justification towards God, and peace*
> *Of Conscience.*
>
> (12. 294–97)

The impossibility of civil justice makes it all the more obvious that individuals must live righteously, according to their own sense of *iustitia,* and look to the kingdom of Christ for the just community. And, as Adam learns, this will not come until God cleanses the earth of sin's pollution: "till fire purge all things new, / Both Heav'n and Earth, wherein the just shall dwell" (11. 900–901).

In *Paradise Lost* the difference between the kingdoms of the fallen world and of heaven, whether heaven is considered as Jerusalem or paradise, is the difference between confusion and peace. The names of the opposing cities contain their own explanation; as Augustine put it, "Babylon confusio interpretatur, Jerusalem visio pacis."[22] Both Augustine and Milton regarded the building of Babel as an egregious example of human presumption and seem to have found the confusion of tongues and God's subsequent scattering of the people a powerful image of the disunity of mankind. To Traherne this confusion signified man's separation from God:

> Truly there are two Worlds, One was made by God, the other by Men. That made by GOD, was Great and Beautifull. Before the Fall, It was Adams Joy, and the Temple of his Glory. That made by men is a Babel of Confusions: Invented Riches, Pomps and Vanities. Give all (saith Thomas a Kempis) for all. Leav the one that you may enjoy the other.[23]

Although Milton did not take Traherne's meditational way of returning to our first world, he surely came to see the cities built by men, with their proliferation of customs and riches, as emblems of the confusion that diverts our attention from the source of all truth and goodness.

Beelzebub summarizes his argument for taking over the earth and turning man against God in these terms:

> *This would surpass*
> *Common revenge, and interrupt his joy*
> *In our Confusion, and our Joy upraise*
> *In his disturbance.*
>
> (2. 370–73)

22. *Ennarationes in Psalmos, Patrologia Latina,* ed. J. P. Migne, 36:773.
23. *Centuries,* 1.7, p. 5.

Milton's syntax here ironically suggests that the fallen angels are themselves living in confusion. Actually, in their alienation from God, their internal discord (before Beelzebub's speech unites the assembly), and their restlessness, they embody the kinds of confusion Satan introduced into the life of man. They find no consolation in philosophizing ("in wandring mazes lost" [2. 561]) or in exploring the bewildering terrain of hell (" In confus'd march forlorn" [2. 615]).

Richard Sibbes's summary of the consequences of the Fall explains very well the dimensions of the confusion Milton attempted to portray. According to Sibbes, "First, there is a skattering and a division from God; the Fountaine of good, with whom we had Communion in our first creation," then "a separation between the good angels and man," then a division between man and other creatures, and finally a division between man and himself.[24] In Chapter 1 above, I discussed Milton's preoccupation with the division between man and God and man and the angels. In Book 10, Milton pictures the "Discord" between man and the creatures and the discord between man and the forces of nature. Man's inner confusion is suggested by the tempest of passions that follows the Fall (9. 1120–26) and Adam's anguished soliloquy in Book 10.[25]

24. *Light from Heaven* (London, 1638), pp. 253ff.

25. Sibbes saw this kind of division as arising from a consciousness of sin: "Where God opens their conscience, there is a hell in their hearts and soules," *Light from Heaven,* p. 254. Compare Donne (*Sermons,* ed. Evelyn Simpson [Berkeley, 1953–62], 4:444) on the Babylon within fallen man. He speaks of "The civil war, the rebellious disorder, the intestine confusion of his own concupiscences. This is a transmigration, a transportation laid upon us all, by Adam's rebellion, from Jerusalem to Babylon, from our innocent state in our creation, to this confusion of our corrupt nature."

The discord between man and man, as embodied in images of violence and injustice, is my concern here. Beginning in Cain's murder of Abel ("th'unjust the just hath slain" [11. 455]), this discord spreads until all earthly relations seem to be based upon "hellish hate." The tyranny exercised by Nimrod and his many successors is simply a more sophisticated form of oppression than the "Sword-Law" of the giants. The splendor of Babylon and the other imperial cities named by Milton in *Paradise Lost* and *Paradise Regained* disguises the fact that they grew strong by war and perpetuated their rule by tyranny. Milton's bitter aside on war in Book 2 suggests that he saw no hope of social harmony in the power of states and empires. Although God offers grace and proclaims peace, men foolishly and irrationally,

> *live in hatred, enmity and strife*
> *Among themselves, and levie cruel warres,*
> *Wasting the Earth, each other to destroy.*
> (2. 500–502)

It is not surprising that Milton described the "horrible confusion" of Chaos largely in terms of human warfare. Chaos can be understood as a nightmarish vision of the anarchic disorder of war as well as a component of Milton's universe. The forces over which Chaos presides are those unleashed by earthly wars:

> Rumor *next and* Chance,
> *And* Tumult *and* Confusion *all imbroild,*
> *And* Discord *with a thousand various mouths.*
> (2. 965–67)

Human violence does not produce disorder on quite this scale, but it mirrors the confusion of the "endless wars" of the atoms. Seen as a maelstrom of forces over which man has no control, war loses all the romance that it has in traditional epics and becomes a terrifying negation of the tranquil social order of heaven. Milton gave a powerful visual statement of this opposition at the close of Book 2, where Satan emerges from the turbulence and din of Chaos to see in the distance heaven's radiant towers and battlements, serene and inaccessible.

Augustine described the Jerusalem of Psalms as "that Jerusalem unto whose peace we are running":[26]

> Who would not long for that City whence no friend goeth out, whither no enemy entereth, where is no tempter, no seditious person, no one dividing God's people, no one wearying the Church in the service of the Devil. . . . There shall be peace made pure in the sons of God, all loving one another, seeing one another full of God, since God shall be all in all.[27]

Milton's New Jerusalem is the poetic expression of a similar vision of peace. The concord of the angels, once Satan and his rebels have been expelled, suggests the sort of harmony with each other and with God that the saints can expect to enjoy. The only kind of genuine peace possible in human society, as Milton describes it in *Paradise Lost* and *Paradise Regained*, is the inner peace of the righteous man. Thomas Adams, the celebrated Puritan preacher, explained the relationship between these two kinds of peace in elaborating on Paul's injunc-

26. *Expositions on the Book of Psalms*, p. 620.
27. Ibid., p. 407.

tion to the Corinthians, "Live in peace, and the God of peace shall be with you":

> For seeking the peace of Earth, wee shall finde peace in Heaven: for keeping the peace of God, we shall be kept by the God of peace. The one is the regular Compasse of our life on Earth, the other is the glorious Crowne of our life in Heaven.[28]

In *Paradise Regained* Christ insists that true glory is not won by the kings and emperors cited by Satan but by the just man who lives in peace:

> *Without ambition, war, or violence;*
> *By deeds of peace, by wisdom eminent,*
> *By patience, temperance; I mention still*
> *Him whom thy wrongs with Saintly patience born,*
> *Made famous in a Land and times obscure;*
> *Who names not now with honour patient* Job?
> (3. 90–95)

As in *Paradise Lost* Milton's emphasis is on individual righteousness and not the collective goodness of a just society. This he had come to see as an unattainable ideal.

A more optimistic view of society emerges from the early antiprelatical tracts. In *Of Reformation* Milton anticipated that England would by completing her reformation enjoy the peace to which she had shown others the way. She would finally "settle the pure worship of God in his Church, and justice in the State."[29] The enthusi-

28. *Eirenopolis: The Citie of Peace* (London, 1630), p. 956.

29. CE, 3, pt. 1:61. See Michael Fixler, *Milton and the Kingdoms of God* (Evanston, 1964), chap. 3, for an extended discussion of the apocalypticism of the early prose.

astic prayer in *Animadversions* suggests how close Milton felt the "shortly expected" kingdom of Christ on earth to be at that point:

> When thou hast settl'd peace in the Church, and righteous judgment in the Kingdome, then shall all thy Saints addresse their voyces of joy, and triumph to thee. . . . Come forth out of thy Royall Chambers, O Prince of all the Kings of the earth, put on the visible roabes of thy imperiall Majesty, take up that unlimited Scepter which thy Almighty Father hath bequeath'd thee; for now the voice of thy Bride calls thee, and all creatures sigh to bee renew'd.[30]

The story of the evolution of Milton's thought—from the expectation of a holy community on earth to a preoccupation with individual liberty and conscience—is too complex to attempt to summarize here.[31] But Milton was still praying for the kingdom of Christ to come when he assumed the task of defending regicide by showing the confidently pictured Charles struck down by God's own "Sword of Justice."[32] Denunciations of the king in *The Tenure of Kings and Magistrates* and *Eikonoklastes* are part of a general attack on the idea of kingship in which Milton invoked the ultimate authority of Revelation:

30. CE, 3, pt. 1:148.
31. See especially Fixler, *Milton and the Kingdom of God;* Arthur Barker, *Milton and the Puritan Dilemma, 1641–1660* (Toronto, 1956); Don M. Wolfe, *Milton in the Puritan Revolution* (New York, 1941).
32. In *The Tenure of Kings and Magistrates*, CE, 5:57.

> But what patrons they be, God in the Scripture oft anough hath exprest; and the earth itself hath too long groand under the burd'n of their injustice, disorder, and irreligion. Therefore "to bind thir Kings in Chaines, and thir Nobles with links of Iron," is an honour belonging to his Saints; not to build *Babel* (which was *Nimrods* work, the first King, and the beginning of his Kingdom was Babel) but to destroy it, especially that spiritual *Babel:* and first to overcome those European Kings, which receive thir power, not from God, but from the beast; and are counted no better than his ten hornes.[33]

In *Paradise Lost* Milton showed, though not with the same fiery zeal, a whole host of kings and their cities, scattered through history and ranging beyond the boundaries of western Europe, to be subject to this final judgment. Yet in the epic his concern is less with the battle of the righteous against their oppressors than with the imperfection of all men. Although in 1660 Milton was still arguing for a "free commonwealth" of just and wise men as an alternative to monarchy, he had seen the collapse of England's experiment with a commonwealth, and his optimism had turned to scorn:

> And what will they at best say of us, and of the whole *English* name, but scoffingly, as of that foolish builder mentioned by our Saviour, who began to build a tower, and was not able to finish it? Where is this goodly tower of a com-

33. *Eikonoklastes,* CE, 5:306.

> monwealth, which the English boasted they would build to overshaddow kings, and be another *Rome* in the west? The foundation indeed they lay gallantly; but fell into a wors confusion, not of tongues, but of factions, than those at the tower of *Babel;* and have left no memorial to their work behind them remaining, but in the common laughter of Europ.[34]

The comparison is especially ironic in that it links the architects of the commonwealth with the line of empire builders that goes back to Nimrod. Milton's use of the same comparison in his digression on contemporary affairs in the *History of Britain* has the effect of incorporating the failure of the commonwealth into the series of human failures recorded there. It recedes into historical perspective as another evidence of the inability of Englishmen to "govern justlie and prudently in peace."[35]

In *Paradise Lost* Milton turned away from questions of polity to the situation of the individual man in a perverted world, "To good malignant, to bad men benigne" (12. 538). In the longer perspective of the epic particular governments seem exercises in pride or futility; all embody to some degree the confusion of Babylon. Northrop Frye sees Milton as reaching back in *Paradise Lost* beyond the political and religious causes for which he had fought to the ideal of paradise:

> Milton's source told him that although heaven is a city and a society, the pattern established

34. *The Readie and Easie Way to Establish a Free Commonwealth*, CE, 6:117–18.
35. CE, 10:324.

> for man on earth by God was not social but individual, and not a city but a garden.
>
> The ultimate precedent, therefore, in which all other precedents are rooted, is not Utopian but Arcadian, not historical but pastoral, not a social construct but an individual state of mind.[36]

The ultimate precedent for Milton is indeed Arcadian, in his special understanding of Arcadia. And in the sense that paradise made it possible for Adam to enjoy a unique peace and communion with God it does indeed mirror an individual state of mind; Michael's insistence that Adam will find a "paradise within" indicates the overwhelming importance that Milton attached to the individual's relationship to God. But paradise is also a social ideal, a place inhabited by two human beings and a host of angels, where God even pays an occasional visit, we are led to believe. The paradise that fills the earth after the judgment will be a glorious community of all the faithful, "far happier" than the original community of Eden:

> *New Heav'ns, new Earth, Ages of endless date*
> *Founded in righteousness and peace and love,*
> *To bring forth fruits Joy and eternal Bliss.*
>
> (12. 549–51)

Such a state represents the perfection of the "peace with God through Christ" (Rom. 5:1) that the faithful can enjoy in the world and also a communal peace made possible by universal righteousness and universal love. This community, into which Christ will gather all the re-

36. *The Return of Eden* (Toronto, 1965), p. 114.

deemed scattered throughout the world and throughout history, will become one with the community of heaven described by Raphael, man joining the angels in bliss.

Although heaven can be thought of as a city and a kingdom that will replace the corrupt cities and kingdoms of the earth, life there bears no relationship to life in earthly cities. The angels serve God out of love, not because of the threat of law or force, and they share equally in the "Joy and eternal Bliss" that spring from the peace of heaven. If heaven is a *civitas,* it is one that has become indistinguishable from paradise. Milton saw that heaven was in fact both city and paradise, combining perfect social order with the ultimate personal happiness. The contrary claims of individual and society are reconciled in the peace of God.

Thomas Adams' remarkable vision of the "mysticall City of Peace" suggests how easily the images of city and paradise could fuse:

> All her Garments are greene and orient. . . . Her breath is sweeter than the new blowen Rose . . . and the smell of her garments is like the smell of *Lebanon.* Her smiles are more reviving than the Vertumnall Sunne-shine: and her favours like seasonable dewes, spring up flowers and fruits wheresoever she walks. . . . Her *Court* is an Image of Paradise: all her Channels flow with milke, and her Conduits runne wine. Envy and murmuring, as privy to their owne guilt, flee from her presence. Her *Guard* consists not of men, but of Angels: and they pitch their Tents about her Palace. Lastly, having preferred and blessed all her

> children on earth, she goes with them to heaven; is welcomed into the armes of her Father, invested Queene with a Diadem of glory, and possessed of those joyes, unto which Time shall never put an End.[37]

One needs to be reminded that this is the peroration of a Puritan sermon and not the final tableau of an unusually ornate Jonsonian masque. The descent of "meek-ey'd Peace" in *On the Morning of Christ's Nativity* represents a comparable if less extravagant venture into the allegorical mode. But in *Paradise Lost* the figure of Peace is replaced by Christ, "the only peace / found out for mankind under wrauth" (3. 274–75). He will lead the redeemed into heaven to see the face of God, "wherein no cloud / Of anger shall remain, but peace assur'd, / And reconcilement" (3. 262–64). The community that they will find there reflects an ideal of social harmony that is pastoral as well as biblical. In *Lycidas* Milton transformed the pastoral ideal of friendship in his brief reference to the "blest Kingdoms meek of joy and love" where the risen Lycidas enjoys a purer and more festive kind of fellowship than he did as a shepherd. In similar fashion, the fellowship of Adam and Eve with each other and with the angels in paradise yields to the prospect of a more festive and joyous fellowship among the saints in heaven.

With his reference to "golden days, fruitful of golden deeds" (3. 337), Milton invited a comparison between the peace of the heavenly community and the peace that Virgil imagined returning to earth with the return of Astraea, or Justice, in the new golden age inaugurated by

37. *Eirenopolis,* p. 1015.

Augustus. The difference illustrates how difficult it is to compare the society of the blessed with any kind of earthly community, even the ideal one imagined by Virgil. In its anticipation of a renewal of justice on earth the ode on the nativity is very like Virgil's messianic eclogue in spirit: "Yea Truth, and Justice then / Will down return to men." This early vision of a universal peace established by the reign of Christ embraces both the classical notion of a restored golden age and the psalmist's anticipation of the salvation of Israel:

*Mercy and Truth that long were miss'd*
*Now joyfully are met;*
*Sweet Peace and Righteousness have kiss'd*
*And hand in hand are set.*
*Truth from the earth like to a flowr*
*Shall bud and blossom then,*
*And Justice from her heavenly bowr*
*Look down on mortal men.*[38]

Christ's reign figures in the vision of the future that Michael grants to Adam, but the ideal of justice on earth does not have the same kind of importance that it does in the ode. In *Paradise Lost* heaven furnishes the model for all visions of order and bliss. We are told that earth will be like heaven, that it will be united with heaven. The dominant idea is that of the peace to be found in heaven, where the concept of justice will cease to have meaning. When God's justice is completed with the act

38. Psalm 85, as paraphrased by Milton. See Rosemond Tuve's excellent discussion of the relationship between the nativity ode and Virgil's fourth eclogue and of Milton's use of Psalms 85 and 89, in *Images and Themes in Five Poems by Milton* (Cambridge, Mass., 1957), pp. 60–62.

of judgment, Christ can lay aside his "regal Scepter" (3. 339). Joy and love "triumphing" will create their own order.

In *Paradise Lost* Milton illustrated the truth of Paul's remark, "God is not the author of confusion but of peace" (1 Cor. 14:33), by tracing the origins and proliferation of confusion and then leaving the reader with a reassuring sense of the nature of God's peace: through Michael's lucid explanation of how man can escape his inner confusion through faith and, above all, through exultant visions of the actual peace of heaven. Satan appears as the author of evil and of the confusion that follows in its wake. In its original, and simplest, form this is the violence that disturbs the peace of heaven ("horrid confusion heapt / Upon confusion rose" [6. 668–69]). We see from Christ's decisive victory that Satan succeeds only in involving himself in confusion by his resort to force. He and his startled legions plunge from heaven, in a fall that foreshadows their final defeat,

> *With ruin upon ruin, rout on rout,*
> *Confusion worse confounded.*
> (2. 995–96)

The subtler forms of confusion that Satan introduces into our world occupy Milton's attention throughout much of *Paradise Lost*. One learns only gradually, with Adam, that all man's self-centered quests—for power, or wealth, or knowledge, or sensual satisfaction—must end in confusion, that the very monuments of worldly success are emblems of confusion. Milton provides the "fit" reader with a guide to the manifestations of sin's disordering effects, and all signs point to the only true alternative to confusion: the peace of God.

# INDEX